THE GRAVE SITUATIONS

OF

MY LITHUANIAN ANCE*STORY*

A POST-HOLOCAUST, ANTI-WAR RANT

First Edition

August 2019

Copyright 2019 Aron Gersh

Human Potential Press

ISBN NUMBER

978-0-9516117-5-3

Also available from Amazon, Kindle Direct Publishing

Cover Design and Typesetting: Aron Gersh & Matthew Wallach

Extracts from the translation of the book by Mina And Chaikel Girsh

"The Tears Don't Count The Years"

Translator Hebrew to English version: Veronica Belling

When Soldiers Die on Battlefields…

By Ed McCurdy

(Famous for his song

"Last night I had the strangest dream")

When soldiers die on battlefields,

Leave them where they lay

And let the bright and burning sun

Their torn young flesh decay

Until the stench so fills the air

That all the human race

Must fill their lungs, and gasping, cry

"Disgrace! Disgrace! Disgrace!"

. . .

Almanac Music, New York

Dedication

Dedicated to the memory of all those of the previous generation in my family who died in the Nazi Holocaust.

Dedicated too to all humans planet-wide who so easily get killed for the most stupid of reasons

Special gratitude to my Uncle Chaikel Girsh and his wife Mina (nee Bod) Girsh for finally recording their too-too painful Holocaust experiences fifty-five years after the war.

THE GRAVE

SITUATIONS

OF

MY

LITHUANIAN

ANCESTORY

— *A POST-HOLOCAUST*

ANTI-WAR RANT

CONTENTS

<u>PART ONE</u>

MY JOURNEY TO

MY PARENTS' HOMELANDS

9   HUMANITY'S INHUMANITY TOWARDS HUMANS

11   TRAUMATIC READING

16   MY FATHER'S FAMILY

31   TORN BETWEEN TWO HATERS

39   AUNT MINA: HER STORY
     —The tattered and torn family of mina (nee bod) girsh

61   AUNT MINA IN THE SIALIAI GHETTO

64   MY FATHER'S SIAULIAI-SHAVEL HOME

69   UNCLE CHAIKEL IN DACHAU

73   A BRIEF HISTORY OF UNCLE CHAIKEL IN DACHAU
     CONCENTRATION CAMP

78   MINA'S DEATH MARCH

___

CONTENTS

PART TWO

MY POST-WAR

POST-HOLOCAUST

RANT

87   SCIENTIFIC   PSYCHOLOGY'S   ATTEMPT   AT
       UNDERSTANDING GENOCIDES

96   THE ENEMY —EVIL AND DISGUSTING

111   RUSSIAN MEMORIALS IN LITHUANIA

115   JEWISH CONSPIRACY THEORIES

118   THE SUFFERINGS OF THE LITHUANIANS

121   CONFRONTING THE DESCENDANTS

133   THE HIDING OF CRIMES

136   IN CONCLUSION

140   THE AUTHOR

PART ONE

MY JOURNEY

TO MY PARENTS' HOMELANDS

HUMANITY'S INHUMAN BEHAVIOUR TO HUMANS?

It's inhuman!

What the Nazis did to the Jews, the gypsies, political prisoners, homosexuals, disabled or retarded people, and to anyone considered to be an enemy of their stupid and sickly philosophy.

I travelled to the places, in Lithuania, where my own Jewish family's Holocaust history took place, learned one thing, made one momentous decision: I will never call the horrors that humans inflict on each other as "inhuman".

On the contrary, they are very human!

Most human! Humans are the cruellest, most dangerous species on the planet!

My mother had grown up in a town called Seduva, in the Radviliski district of Lithuania. Her whole nuclear family with six siblings emigrated to South Africa in the 1920's. But the Jews who remained behind in Seduva were slaughtered to the person, all of them, when the Germans entered in 1941.

An old non-Jewish Lithuanian woman, Emilija Brajinskiene, described as a "Holocaust Witness", in an interview for Youtube entitled "The Jews of Seduva", tells this story (translated from the Lithuanian)

"I recall a girl named Rachel, she had a very beautiful doll which could open and close its eyes. Lithuanians did not own such dolls. When the Jews were taken to be shot, Rachel took the doll with her. And after they had been shot . . I don't know when and where Rachel lost the doll . . .
But people would often go to the locations of shootings to see what had become of the Jews. In the trail of tyres someone noticed a baby's hand sticking out of the gravel. When they picked it up, it turned out to be Rachel's doll.

It opened its eyes and started crying!

The person was so deeply affected by it! It was as though they saw Rachel herself."

Must say I felt a bit like that doll, being unearthed to my family's Holocaust past.

Unearthing things that were never spoken about in our families, opening my eyes, to the reality of it, in the places where they actually happened, I cried too . . . like that baby.

TRAUMATIC READING

"Sticks and Stones will break my bones, but words will never hurt me" goes an old rhyme, exhorting us not to be hurt by harsh words from others, only from violent attacks on our bodies. And the fact is, verbal attacks are tame by comparison to attacks which destroy the very instrument of human communication, the body, with its amazing ability to express itself, verbally and by non-verbal communication. But we do get hurt by verbal attacks from others. The fact is, words are powerful . . .

I was watching some YouTube videos from experts who study the Holocaust and who know the vast extent of its horrific human devastation. One expert said: "Reading about the Holocaust is traumatising . . . ".

Reading about the Holocaust is traumatising???

Well, so many of us, empathic human beings, of all races, nations, religions, can and do feel deeply when we read about, or see films about the horrors, the "heart of darkness" (Well, that was the title of a novel by Joseph Conrad depicting horrors within some black, superstitious and paranoid tribes in the Congo. Between 1885 and 1908

King Leopold II of Belgium wreaked unspeakable horrors on the black slave population who were extracting rubber from the rubber trees for Europe's usage. Critics suggest Conrad was clear that "uncivilised behaviour" was spread equally among black folk and white folk — in this case, between black slaves and colonial masters. That destructive human nature is universal, equally spread amongst all the populations of the earth, is an idea that accords solidly with the stance of this book).

I don't think I have ever been *traumatised* by reading about the Holocaust or seeing movies like *Schindler's List.* I feel the horror, and then get back to the present needs of my life. But I have not been able to do that since my visit to Lithuania, my first ever, to the sites where my family suffered, where I could touch the earth of mass graves. I would not describe myself as traumatised. And I am hoping you, dear reader, will not get traumatised either by reading this book of horrors. I am indeed holding back certain true facts which are too gruesome even to read about. But the act of being physically present, where these things actually happened, and the fact that it related so strongly and so intimately to my own direct family, plus my extended family, meant that it sank deeper into my soul than ever before.

And so I have to write this book. I am unable to leave this past behind, unable to say these memories are not important. Because I have time and resources to do this, I need to do it for the sake of healing my own soul, processing these deep feelings, clearing up and "finishing the past" in such a way that I can get on with so many things that are needed in my present life, and future goals. It seems my living extended family want me to do this too.

These past stories, these memories, are like the lives of those few Jews who, only wounded and not quite dead when mass shootings were perpetrated at mass graves, cheated being dead and buried. Gravel and sand were thrown upon them, but they had enough air, enough breath, to survive, rise from the graves, and live again . . . full lives till their natural deaths, some of them. I cannot ignore these voices that refuse to be stilled, these memories that keep surfacing from the soil into my Jewish consciousness. I have to let them live, till they die a natural death.

I live in Cape Town, South Africa. At the end of 2018 I had a book translated from Hebrew to English. My uncle Chaikel, and my aunt Mina, in the year 2000, 55 years after the end of WWII, published a book about their horrific experiences when the Nazis invaded Lithuania and occupied it till the end of the war. There were many names and places in the book. I decided it was time to go there and see, just once in my lifetime, to soak myself in that past, to honour both the survivors and the slaughtered from those terrible times.

I was born exactly after the ending of WWII, and I realised that for all post-war citizens, of all nations, who grew up among those who had actually experienced the war horrors, that we have a responsibility to pass on any knowledge we have of direct actual experiences that that generation might have told to us. I have not a clue how many will read this book. Perhaps only my family, and a few others. But, in the same way that I learned how important it was that aunt Mina and uncle Chaikel had preserved their experiences for future generations, I realised that this is my "post-Holocaust experience" — my telling to future generations that even 70 years after the war was over, its effects still lingered deeply in many of our human hearts, and currently, very deeply in my own. This book is the baton I am passing on to the next generation whom I hope will not drop the baton till the race is over and won.

MY FATHER'S FAMILY

My father's family came from a larger town than my mother, called Siauliai, or Shavel or Shavli, (in the Yiddish and Hebrew tongues). His two older brothers had emigrated, one at a time, as young men, to South Africa, one of few places who would accept Jews. He followed them.

They knew none of the languages there and had to be helped to integrate into the society by the Yiddish speakers who had come before them. The Afrikaners, who let them in, and thus saved our lives, identified strongly with the Jews, seeing them, like themselves, to be the "People of the Book", namely the Bible.

Almost all of the Jewish immigrants to South Africa were Yiddish speaking folk from Lithuania. As kids, we would enter smoke-filled rooms where the men were playing cards, enthusiastically calling their shots in Yiddish terminology; and the women were on the sofas and easy chairs, talking recipes and foods and probably gossiping somewhat too. We understood very little Yiddish as kids, as they used it as a secret language when they did not

---

want us to understand. A little went in by osmosis. That almost killed a whole language in one generation — in favour of the blossoming new secular Hebrew (previously only used for Religion).

The families of the South African Jews who had stayed behind in Lithuania were almost all slaughtered by the Nazis, often with enthusiastic help from Lithuanian locals — some of whom hated Jews and enjoyed the benefits from simply taking properties and goods from deported and slaughtered Jews. Uncle Chaikel, in his book, said there were anti-Jewish movements from 1918 already. And their anti-Jewish sentiments and actions against Jews grew stronger when the Nazis took hold in Germany in 1933. For instance, the "Shaulists" were a right-wing group (white armbands on their upper arms) involved not only in heavy political action against successful Jewish traders, but in attacks of violence against Jews. When the war broke out, they simply, under the protection of the Nazis, helped themselves to Jewish properties and possessions as a nice easy form of enriching themselves.

What a nice form of capitalistic competitive behaviour!

I guess it stems from inferiority feelings —not being able to create that wealth by their own skill and intelligence! Jealousy!

And then they helped with some of the killing of the Jews. There is evidence that some such groups collaborated with the Germans and were heavily involved in the infamous mass killings in the forests of Ponary (Penariai) just outside Vilnius. About 70,000 or more were slaughtered and buried there, mostly Jews (20,000 Poles, and 8000 Russian POW's were killed too. Approximately 100,000 humans in total).

From the roughly 220,000 Jews overall in Lithuania, about 200,000 were massacred, only about 20,000 survived —about 95% of the population, the highest percentage of Jewish annihilation than in any other of the Nazi-occupied countries. In my father's town of about 5,500 Jews, only about 500 survived. In my mother's town, about 550 Jews there before the war, all were slaughtered. 100%!

My generation never quite knew this when we were growing up — how lucky we were to be alive! Had those 3 brothers not emigrated, they too might very well have been murdered. And we would not have been born.

From the 8 children of Grandpa Aron Girsh (who I have been named after) and his wife Golda Miller, 3 of them got caught up in the Nazi animal traps, spent the war years in unbelievable suffering, but survived. The oldest daughter, Rachel, had fallen in love with a radical communist, and before the German invasion, had followed him into Russia. The family had just one letter from her, and then lost all contact forever. The youngest brother, Mayer (Meir), got onto a bicycle when he heard of the German invasion, cycled a long way, and spent the war years safely enough in Russia.

The three who were trapped were my uncle Chaikel, and his two sisters, Rivke and Miriam (also known as Mary). These lived through the hell. Almost anything you might have seen of the basic horrors of what happened, it happened to them. Uncle Chaikel, as a 21-year-old, had fallen in love with one Mina, a 16-year-old who had come to live in the family's crowded house in the Siauliai ghetto. They were separated during the war, for 4 years, but found each other after the war, and married, and produced two lovely daughters —Golda, named after our grandmother, Aron Girsh's wife, and Rachel, named after the daughter who had disappeared into Russia.

The typical burden of children of Holocaust survivors seems to be this, that the attitude of your parents might be:

"Nothing you are experiencing is anything, anything at all, like how bad things could be. Basically, you kids have it all, and complaints about a cold uncomfortable bed, or lack of hot water for a shower for one night, or that this food is not what you quite wanted right now and think you have a right to have exactly what you desire. . .all such complaints are petty, and meaningless. You don't know how good you have it! You have a bed to yourself, a room to yourself, more food than you can eat! What are you crying about!"

It must be hard for some Holocaust parents to realise that children cannot contextualise their own history in this way. They did not have those experiences. They are now! That was then! Nevertheless, it is not such a bad thing for all of us to know how good we have it (if we do) compared to others who are far worse off than us —such awareness can increase our gratitude for the many blessings we do in fact have!

But my uncle and aunt apparently did not at all place such a burden on their children, and, wanting them to have a normal upbringing in Israel, where they had landed up, did not want to burden their kids with the horrors of their past history. But in the late 1990's, the daughters insisted the parents tell and record their tragic histories. So the two parents wrote a book, divided into two parts: His Story, and Her Story. The title, translated from the Hebrew, is "The Tears don't count the Years" . . . meaning, the cries of that past never quieten down, the tears never dry up.

In late 2018 I at last got that book translated from the Hebrew into English, so that I myself, and my English-speaking family could all read it, at last. And, because so many places had been named, pinpointed, I decided I would take me and my bicycle to Lithuania to, at least once in my life, honour the past history of all these recent ancestors . . . both those who had escaped the Holocaust, and those who had not. I did not realise what deep waters of the past I would be swimming in, almost drowning in.

Do we, the generation who came after the bloody horror of our family's demises, have anything meaningful to say, any story to tell, which is worth writing???

Nothing we say or experience can compare with what our families trapped by the Nazis experienced!

So I don't know if anyone will be interested in reading this "next generation" story. I only know I have to write it! If it tells the readers one thing, it is this: that past history lives in our hearts, and still pains us.

It crosses generations!

The ancestors are alive in us!

I want to tell you how!

I never quite realised for how long, and how deeply, this journey would cause me to lose touch with most of things in my life which involved what was needed in present action . . . or what was needed in preparation for future goals. And there was plenty of that. Present problems and future goals were temporarily shelved.

This turned out to be a constant conundrum humming in my head: to what extent shall we live in the past, what extent in the present, and how much should be devoted to the future.

I have two reasons why this conundrum begs an answer in my head. Some of the children from the next generation in our extended family had no interest in reading my uncle and aunt's book. The past for them is dead and buried, and they are very busy with the present and the future. What shall we say of that? Are they entitled to forget about the past, as if it never existed, and just get on with the present and the new, a-historical future?

The other reason is that most of my new-agey friends have been reading Eckhart Tolle, a best-selling mega-star guru whose main book is entitled "The Power of the Present" and who is exhorting us all to live totally in the present, in the here-and-now. Well, certainly, if our personal past is hanging us up, not letting us get on with our personal present and develop towards our unique individual future, then it is important to learn to get past that past, and get to this present, for those who have not arrived here yet.

But there are a whole load of things I just can't quite dig about that philosophy. For one thing, with me about to dig into my family and my nation's historical past, it is clear that, as in art and graphics, "background determines figure", or in language "context determines meaning" — by which I mean my current present derives much of its meaning from the past which it has grown out of, much as the nature of a tree's trunk is highly determined by the nature of its roots.

Tolle had, on his own admission, a very anxious and depressed past, and, understandably, wanted to be free of it. In other words, the only reason he knows his present is "peaceful" is because this current figure shows up against a background past which was "painful and anxious"

And anyway, for those who have had happy pasts, happy memories, shall we exhort them to forget those?

In other words, I have a deep suspicion that Eckhart Tolle tries to live a-historically . . . and has not a clue as to how *real past history* (as opposed to *past philosophies and religions*) provides background and context, gives meaning to the present, that the present cannot be fully known without it, and also that the past can and often should provide direction and purpose as to how the present should be spent to create a certain different, and hopefully better, future. Humans live on a constant time-line, a continuum from past to present to future. What is wrong with:

"Now, in this present time, which is the only place I can ever really be, I choose to remember the past, for all its good and bad; And now, in this present time, I am going to imagine what the future will bring, and what I will bring to the future, for good or bad"

I wonder what he would say about me finding it meaningful right now to go and live in the past for a while.

Uncle Chaikel and his beloved Mina survived the war. Uncle Chaikel had already left school by the time the Germans came, and had time to develop trades, skills the Germans needed. Mina, and the other two girls survived because they still had the energy of youth, hence were needed for their back-breaking labour. But it was all just touch-and-go. Always just touch-and-go!

Grandpa Aron Girsh did not survive. Uncle Chaikel saw him for a last time in an overcrowded hut at the Stutthof concentration camp, just outside Gdansk, Poland, to where they were deported by train from the Siauliai ghetto. The young and fit were sorted and isolated, and he never saw his father again. Grannie Golda never survived either.

You see, this was one of the most heart-breaking things for me, for anyone. Their two girls, Rivka and Mary, had already just married, and each had a child just at the beginning of the war. All that our family in South Africa had later learned about them was that grannie Golda and her two young grandchildren, a boy and a girl, had been deported together to be killed. All my life there was a little space of pain in my heart especially for those two kids.

But I never knew their names!

They would have been my oldest cousins. I imagined that they had a fairly good life in Lithuania, then the Nazis came, took them away, end of story. I always wanted, at least, to honour their memories, by knowing their names.

So as a young man I visited Israel for the first time and visited aunty Rivke there. I broached the subject, having tea with her. She got up and backed out of the door of the lounge as if she had been confronted by a monster. "We don't talk about these things!!! We talk about happy things", she commanded pleadingly, fear popping out of her eyes.

Years later she was living with her sons, the two she had after the war, in the Poconos in America and I visited them there — my two first cousins and their mum Rivke. She was 91. How a human body goes through all that Holocaust trauma with all its hunger and bodily abuse and still manages to repair itself adequately to live to a ripe old age, I will never know. But the sons told me that "These days she speaks more openly about the past".

I came to breakfast the first morning there. Aunty Rivke came to sit with me, and, to my great surprise, calling me by my Yiddish diminutive name, said: "Aronele, do you know I had a daughter . . . "

My God! I could hardly believe what I was hearing: "I know, I know, Aunty Rivke. What was her name???", I asked expectantly.

"Sarah . . . Sarele" (Little Sarah, just as Aronele is Yiddish for Little Aron)

That was a momentous moment in my life!

But I did not prod my aunt for details.

Such is my post-Holocaust story!

And I still did not know the little boy's name. Aunty Mary, his mother, has died years ago . . . relatively young by comparison, though she too did manage to produce one bonny boy in America after the war.

Thank you Uncle Chaikel and Aunty Mina for writing your book, "The Tears don't count the Years" in the year 2000. What happened to grannie Golda and the children is captured in the genocide history books as "the terrible day that they came for the children". Not that there was just one such day. But there was one such day in the ghetto in Siauliai-Shavel. It is described in uncle and aunt's book and in many of the historic accounts. It happened on 5th November 1943.

You have probably seen movies or read stories about that. The mothers had been marched out of the ghetto to go to their work places. Then the packs of murderous beasts gathered around the ghetto in a major roundup — or what was called an "Aksion". You probably know how the Nazis piled children on trucks as if they were firewood, threw them from rooftops if they had been hiding, or butted them with their rifles, and I won't say more . . .

As far as we know, Grannie Golda chose to go with them, and that they were taken to Auschwitz. The boy's name, which I had never known, was Moses, or, in Yiddish, Moishe, and, being little, Moishele.

Moishele and Sarele!

My heart always breaks when I think about you!

You could not have been born at a worse time!

You spent the biggest portion of your life in a ghetto, must have always been hungry, and then were taken to the slaughter . . .

My heart will never not ache when I think of you . . . as it does now, as I write about it.

<u>Such is my post-Holocaust story!</u>

So that was "the day they came for the children"? But what about babies . . . what happened to babies??? Well, there are so many horror stories about babies, that I truly find them traumatising, and will not traumatise my readers with them. But here is one I will let uncle Chaikel describe in his own words from the book:

On 7 February 1942, in addition to all the other existing prohibitions, they issued an order that it was forbidden to give birth in the ghetto. The last date that it was allowed to give birth was 15 August 1942. If there were to be a birth in a Jewish family after that date the whole family would be killed. Pregnant women could choose between bringing forward the birth or killing the foetus. Doctors who refused to perform abortions on account of conscience left the decision in the hands of the mother. With no other option there were parents who drowned their own babies and did not allow them to stay alive, knowing that if they did not do this themselves, the Germans would not only kill the baby but would also kill them and their entire family. One or two women dared to give birth in secret and smuggled their babies out of the ghetto by giving them to gentiles.

Note that the order only allowed 6 months and one week for potential parents to implement it!!! Well-organised line-up of guaranteed slaughter party by the Nazi Heartless idiots!

TORN BETWEEN TWO HATERS

Both uncle Chaikel and Aunt Mina in their separate experiences of the beginning of the occupation by the Germans, tell of the substantial and interminable help a substantial portion of the local Lithuanians who hated Jews gave to the Germans:

When the Russians retreated in the face of the Germans at the time of the occupation, there were Jews who fled with them. Then it was still easier to flee; my brother Meir, for example, fled on his bicycle. There were also those who were unfortunate and who were caught by the Shaulists in the Lithuanian Guard. Five friends that I knew, one of them Pozrinski Shlomo, played with me in the Maccabi football team as a goalkeeper, three of the Polish refugees – tried to flee, but were caught by the Lithuanian partisans, and they were the ones who murdered them, not the Germans. The Germans never spoke the local language and could not easily identify Jews by their outer appearance. But the Lithuanians did their work for them and they used to lock up Jews who hid away or who fled.

I grew up with a song "Torn between two lovers", about a woman who loved two men equally, and felt torn by that fact. It seems that in Lithuania the Jews were torn between two "haters". They were generally seen as being on the wrong side.

In the first World War, my mother used to tell me, the Jews were sent from Lithuania inland into Russia, because the Tsarist war with Germany meant that the Russians were scared the Jews, whose Yiddish language resembled the German language closely, could too easily give support, or even spy for, the Germans. Uncle Chaikel, my dad's younger brother, also mentions this in his book.

At the start of WWII Lithuania had about one year under the rule of the Russians. Many Jews were indeed in favour of the caring-for-the-workers Communist philosophy (I don't know if they had a clue about the Fascism that would arise from this political movement in Russia). Thus, when the Germans invaded Lithuania in 1941, the Jews were seen as potential supporters and potential spies for the Russians . . . apart from the fact that they, like a whole group of other nations, were seen as unter-menschen (sub-humans).

Actually, as I write it strikes me there is a strange irony in the different use of the word "Mensch" in German and its use in Yiddish. Of course, literally it simply means "a person". But for Jews, even today for those who know little Yiddish, a "Mensch" is a person who is a really fine person, a good person, a kind person, a gentle person — a real gentleman, if male.

For the German Nazis an "unter-mensch" referred to a sub-human being.

Dear German Nazis, may I suggest that, in the Yiddish meaning of the word, it is thou who were all "unter-Menschen" (sub-decent human beings).

Of course, not all Jews could agree with the communist viewpoint that religion was a bad thing. It seems to me thus that religious Jews did not subscribe to Communism, or if they did, I do not know how they would have reconciled with its anti-religious philosophy. Many of the Jews who were inclined to Communism were atheists, but who, to the best of my limited knowledge, created nontheistic forms of maintaining their Jewish traditions. I recently heard a lecturer who told us that a popular song we sing at Passover (Pesach) was rewritten with words associated with the oppression (and seeking freedom) of factory labourers. She also told us about the vast numbers of Jews who subscribed to Anarchism —non-hierarchical "government".

But I wonder about how a nation, any nation, gets to be seen as an enemy within.

Why could the Jews not be seen as a Blessing within the country instead of as a curse?

They had excellent skills, excellent education, some of the best doctors and intellectuals. Generally they brought wealth and trade to the places they were scattered to.

For example, the famous Frenkel factories in Siauliai brought enormous wealth to the city. Frenkel was giant of a business magnate in Europe generally, and specifically created the Frenkel Palace and Frenkel Villa which one can still see in Siauliai-Shavel. He had made his millions because he and his scientists had created a sole for military shoes which was far longer-lasting than any that had been designed to date. The Russian, Tsarist army, bought millions of these, and so Frenkel got rich. He created a major tannery in Siauliai, a leather-works that produced all sorts of amazing products.

Interestingly, when the Germans took over the factory, and got rid of the Jewish skilled and unskilled workers there and substituted them with local Lithuanian workers, productivity suffered so much, so that the new German bosses saw to it that the original Jewish workers were brought back in again.

Jewish unter-menschen ?

Instead of deprecating them, why can't the majority population appreciate them?

It seems as if these days many European nations are beginning to see that they were denuded of a very creative, very valuable bunch of people —the Jews. And now, with scientific testing of Intellectual Quotient (IQ), it has been established beyond a doubt, even by right wing racist scientists, that Ashkenazi Jews have average IQ's (Intelligence Quotients) one whole standard deviation above the normal (for every normal population curve there are 3 standard deviations above zero and 3 below zero). Jewish unter-menschen?

And while we are on that subject, in Germany before WWII, Jews were about 1% of the population, but getting a vastly out-of-proportion share of the Nobel prizes. I don't know the exact figure, but Wikipaedia tells us this:

> Nobel prizes have been awarded to over 900 individuals, of whom at least 20% were Jews, although the Jewish population comprises less than 0.2% of The world's population. Various theories have been made to explain this phenomenon, which has received considerable attention.

I asked a Holocaust world expert at Israel's Yad Vashem museum to the Holocaust how the Germans squared this fact with Jews as unter-menschen. His reply, to put it simply, was "no rationality" . . . I guess those Nazis were extra dumb, not being able to see what was clearly a fact in front of their eyes in Germany itself. Humans see what they want to see, don't see what they don't want to. And often simply project their own reality onto areas of life which are vague until we apply serious clear-seeing instruments to see what is really going on.

Unter-menschen?

Who were really the Untermenschen?

It was a case of real human beings being Untermensch-lich!

At any rate, note how easy it was for the two countries, Germany and Russia, to perceive Jews as "the enemy within": The Russians in WWI saw them as pro-German, because they had a similar language to the Germans. The Germans saw them as pro-Communist, as part of their enemies, the Communists. The Russians saw the Jews as pro-Religion, and therefore as enemies of the Russian atheistic philosophy. In some places they saw them as richer and more educated, unlike struggling farmers, and therefore as "bourgeoisie", hence as the enemy within.

Well, presumably some Jews were pro-Communist, but pro-Religion, some pro-Communist, but anti-Religion too. Some were anti-Communist. The very assimilated "enlightened" Jews of Germany before the Nazis were probably in some way pro-German.

Humans can pluck out one or two qualities from some individuals in a complex societal group and generalise those qualities to the whole group, decide on what those qualities mean and then act on the whole group as if it has all those qualities and as if those qualities mean what they are thought to mean— as in WWI:

"Jews can speak with Germans because they have a similar language; therefore all Jews are potential spies" — even though no Jews of Lithuania were, to the best of my knowledge, at all pro-German. In South Africa, our Lithuanian Jewish parents were somewhat judgmental of even the *German Jews* there, because they were too much like the Germans, too 'integrated'.

The point is that you can find a wide variety of people within every society and thus, seeking a particular enemy, with particular qualities, you can find a few there . . . and then you can generalise these to that whole population even if they constitute a very small percentage of that population.

Pow! In one simple fell swoop, you have found a million enemies in your midst — and that is a good enough excuse to abuse and torture them. The ones in the group who do not at all have those "inimical qualities" are simply lumped in with those who do —major overgeneralisation.

Seriously dumb, unthinking behaviour — so very human!

AUNT MINA -HER STORY

Aunt's Mina's family came from a town, Telsiai (Lithuanian) or Telz (Yiddish) about 45 miles (70 kilometres) from Uncle Chaikel's larger town of Siauliai (Shavel). There were lots of Jewish educational institutes there, for instance, a Jewish Yeshiva, and she went to one Yavneh girl's Jewish school.

But when she was 16, the Nazis came to town (June 1941), and changed all her young dreams of what she was going to achieve in a splendidly lived life. She used to, in the years after the war, wake up from bad dreams about the past, wake up sobbing. These days we call it *Post Traumatic Stress Reaction*. How can one not be affected by going through those horrors! ```

Some historical background first.

The Russians had occupied free Lithuania about a year earlier, 7 June 1940. You must understand that this was due to a secret pact that had occurred between Germany and Russia in 1939, the Molotov-Ribbentrop Pact. It was denied long after the war but was eventually admitted to by the Russians. The pact suggested how

Germany and Russian were going to carve up the states between their two powerful countries — the Baltic states, Czechoslovakia, Poland, Belarus etc. Lithuania had been promised to Russia and they occupied it in 1940 and nationalised all private enterprises. This ostensible "peace pact" between Germany and Russia was just a ruse for the manipulative, psychopathic, lying Hitler, and on 20 June 1941 Germany began their fast occupation of Lithuania. Operation Barbarossa! The largest invasion force in the history of warfare!

At first it looked like the Russians were going to contain the Nazi forces, but soon the German might was overwhelming. Wikipaedia describes it as folows:

Over the course of the operation, about three million personnel of the Axis Powers—the largest invasion force in the history of warfare —invaded the western Soviet Union along a 2,900-kilometer (1,800 mi) front. In addition to troops, the Wehrmacht deployed some 600,000 motor vehicles, and between 600,000 and 700,000 horses for non-combat operations. The offensive marked an escalation of

World War II, both geographically and in the formation of the Allied Coalition.

My God! All that money and gargantuan resources spent on useless wars! Imagine if that money had been usefully spent, how it could have enriched the beleaguered German nation. I learnt at school that Germany went to war because it was struggling economically as a result of harsh settlements at the end of WWI. So, someone, please explain to me: how does such a poor, struggling nation have resources to put the largest invasion force in the history of warfare into action???

And how can one blame any victimised citizens for being too fearful to organise armed resistance to such an overwhelmingly powerful animal trap. This information gives me the greatest respect for all and any freedom fighters, who had little chance against all this.

This enormous force was available because from the 10th May 1940 the Nazis had, in 6 weeks, conquered the western front, France, Belgium, the Netherlands and so on. They were free to concentrate on the Eastern front, to head towards Russia, and one prong of the attack was through Lithuania.

So the Russians began retreating, back over Latvia, and towards Russia. The independent partisans of Lithuania cheered the arrival of the Germans because they saw them as liberators from the Russians. Many individual reports tell us that the Germans were greeted with cheers and flowers. As some Jews were serious socialists, concerned about the plights of the oppressed working classes, and often were "card-carrying" communists, they were hated by the Lithuanians for being pro-Russian, and who quickly wrote themselves onto the same page as the Nazis . . . and many started abusing and even killing Jews. They shot at the retreating Russian army, often assassinating Russian military personnel in their cars.

Aunt Mina's family, like many others, having heard that the Germans were hunting Jews, followed the paths of the retreating Russian soldiers. Her own words:

When we left the house, we did not take anything with us except a jar filled with cherries sweetened with juice. For days and nights we wandered along the road with many other Jews. Lithuanian gangs, who called themselves, "Partisans", shot at the soldiers of the Red Army as they were retreating, stopped the cars of the

42

families of the Soviet officers and murdered them. They also shot at the Jews who were fleeing, who were murdered by these bands, who did not wait for the arrival of the Germans but on their own initiative enthusiastically perpetrated the murderous deeds.

But their retreat was in vain. They discovered that the Germans had already entered Latvia, the next country, and blocked off their retreat. There was no escape, and they might as well just head back home.

But, as some of the Lithuanian soldiers, and civilians too, had joined the German hunt for Jews, their lives were in constant danger, and they tried to approach home in Telz (Telsiai) with as little visibility as possible, often in forests. They had heard about the massacre in a suburb of Kaunas (Kovno). Wikipaedia tells us:

The most infamous incident occurred in the Lietukis garage, where several dozen Jewish men were publicly tortured and executed on June 27, most of them killed by a single club-wielding assailant nicknamed the "Death Dealer."

Meanwhile back in Telz, all the remaining Jews were uprooted and taken to the Rainiai forest (Mina calls it the "Rein" forest, or "Royin" forest, in the Yiddish dialect), at the Rainiai farm, just 2 miles out of town. When Mina's family were caught by the Lithuanian "partisans", they too were taken to that forest and housed in stables.

Mina tells us:

As soon as we arrived in terror, turmoil and with broken hearts, we were told hair-raising tales of what had happened in the forest during our absence. The murderous deeds were accompanied by cruel savagery and destruction of property, that continued for days, under the supervision of German commando units (mostly made up of Lithuanian "white armbands" or "Sha'ulistim," as they were called). One morning the men were brought to the diggings that were prepared for the armoured corps, and there they were shot to death. And also in Royin we found a camp of women and children and a small number of men. There was virtually not a single family that had been spared the orphaning and for whom this was not a part of their lot.

They were kept in the quarters of the cattle under terrible conditions that were not even worthy of their occupants. The Lithuanians continued collecting Jews from the villages round about and bringing them to the Royin forest. It was not long before the men who still remained were sacrificed. Like those who came before them, one day they were brought to the diggings where they were killed. There in the Royin forest they went on their final journey and reached the gates of death together with the masses of the House of Israel.

Mina's father and youngest brother were murdered there (Her older brother Zalman, like Chaikel was away with the Lithuanian army).

When I was in Telz I took a cycle ride down to the Rainiai (Royin) forest. There was a sign to the Jewish memorial but following that forest path I found only Christian memorials. Then, up the road was a magnificent memorial chapel, looming at a high point in that half-forested countryside.

The inscription on it read:

Rainiai Chapel is built to commemorate one of the most tragic events in Lithuania history during the last week of events of the first Soviet occupation and of the massacre in Rainiai forest during the night of June 24-25, 1941. Soviet soldiers with local collaborators, sadistically murdered <u>74 Lithuanian political prisoners:</u> teachers, students, farmers, tradespeople, officers and workers from Tesiai, Plunge and Kretinga district. The <u>biggest "crimes" they committed</u> were love for the homeland and unwillingness to obey occupants.

Their biggest crimes were love for their homeland, and unwillingness to obey occupants . . . !

Every life killed is a universe killed, and I bow my head in sorry for these terrible "enemies of the (Soviet) state" who wanted nothing more than freedom for their own homeland, and not to have to bow to the dictates of a foreign force. But why were the non-Jewish Lithuanian memorials so visible and accessible, but not the Jewish

———

Lithuanian memorials — because I knew that somewhere in the forest was a memorial to the many Jewish victims. In fact, there are photos of more than just one memorial stone . . .

Then in my research on Jewish Genealogy, I found a story about the Jewish men in the Rainiai forest before they were slaughtered.

After eight days the men were taken to work, their first task being to dig up from their graves the corpses of 74 political prisoners who had been imprisoned in Telz prison and had been murdered by Soviet security men before they withdrew. Under the pretext that Jews had taken part in that murder, the Telz men were forced to wash the corpses, to kiss them and lick the decayed wounds. The thirty Jewish men who were the victims of this abuse, having been beaten and wounded, were forced later to kneel in the street during the funeral of the murdered. The Catholic Bishop Staugaitis proclaimed the day of the funeral, July 13, as "Holy Sunday", to symbolize victory over Soviet Rule.

Seems like there are two sides to every story . . .and notice that some of the "locals" who helped the Soviets were Lithuanians who did not take the side of the Nazis, but joined the Communists. Ah, how easy is it to find a suitable enemy when one needs one!

I never did find the Jewish memorial sites, where, according to the photo on the headstone I researched, about 7000 Jews had been murdered.

7000!

And hard to find even a sign leading you to the memorial!

The "biggest crimes they committed were"???

Competing fairly with other cultures?

Well here is some outside information about the men at Rainiai: (from Jewishgen.org "Preserving our Litvak heritage". (Litvak = Yiddish for Lithuanian).

On the 14th of July several Germans and Lithuanians appeared in the camp, driving all from the sheds and barns. The women and children were returned to the sheds, but the men were forced to run in a circle, fall down and stand up, while Lithuanians armed with sticks stood around, scourging them and hitting them all over their bodies. Many of the Telz residents came to see "the special show" and clapped. Several elderly Jews died there and then, the others, smitten and wounded, were put back into barns.

80 young and strong Jewish men were then taken from there, given shovels and buckets, and led to a nearby grove where pits already existed. They were forced to pump the water out of the pits, then they were shot and thrown into the pits. The shooting was heard at the camp, but the prisoners did not realize what was going on. During the night the Lithuanians came to the camp, demanding 24 men more for work, and after a short while shooting was heard again.

The next day, June 15, 1941 (20th of Tamuz 5701) all men were taken out of the camp, and led, in groups, to the grove and murdered. They were forced to undress and stand on a plank which was put across the pit, and there they were shot. Many fell into the pit unhurt, and thus buried alive. In the afternoon a big rain storm erupted, and the shooting stopped. Those men still alive were ordered to retrieve some garments from the pile, to dress and run to the shacks, where they were concentrated in one of them. Some managed to infiltrate into the women's shack and disguise themselves as women, but the next morning the killing continued, including the disguised men. The rabbis, whose beards were cut off or plucked off together with the skin of their faces, were in the last group.

Before the shooting the men were forced to take off their clothes, the good clothes being taken by the murderers for themselves and the rest brought to the camp. The women recognized the garments of their husbands and in them even photos of themselves and their children, and a great cry arose. In the nights the Lithuanian guards would burst into the barns and frighten the women, many of whom were raped.

Several days after the murder, the thin layer of soil which covered the corpses at the graves, started to crack and a terrible stench enwrapped the area.

This may have been one of the reasons for transferring the women to Geruliai camp, about 10 km from Telz.

On July 22 Lithuanians appeared in Rainiai camp, announcing that in a few hours all women and children would be transferred to the Geruliai camp. Most of these miserable women had to walk on foot, carrying their few belongings to the new camp, with only a few being taken on carts. Before the transfer several SS men with Lithuanians arrived in Rainiai camp and ordered the women to hand over their leather handbags, shoes, boots etc. and also any money they still had.

Yeh! All that historical description fits my aunt Mina's story exactly. She tells us that after the murder of all the men in the Royin forest, the women and children were taken to a forest called the Girul (Geruliai) forest. About 4000 Jews were stuffed into stables there with almost no food and certainly no medical facilities. Then one day the Germans asked all the women aged 15 to 35 to report for parade. They were going to be marched back to the Telz (Telsiai) ghetto. The older women and children, they were told, would be brought later on vehicles.

In Mina's own words from the book:

One day it happened — it seems to me to have been in August 1941 — that we were ordered to report for an inspection on the parade on the field next to the stables. An order was issued that all of the women between the ages of 15-35 should leave the camp. It was announced that they were taking us to the Telz Ghetto, and that they would bring the older people, such as my mother, who was at the time about 43 years old, and the children in a vehicle later on, because they were talking of a distance of several kilometres.

I stood in the square with my mother and my siblings; my brother Uri would be celebrating his barmitzvah soon. My mother, like myself, apparently believed that we would meet again. She told us to go and later they would join us. We never in our heart of hearts believed that we would never meet again. About 500 women left, amongst them my sister Devora, Inga and I. Mother remained standing with my younger siblings, Uri, Aharon and Ita – while my sister Devora and I together with all the other young people that were taken out of the camp, organised ourselves in lines.

While we were still walking to the Telz Ghetto, a distance of some two to three kilometres from the Girul camp, we heard the sound of shots coming from the camp that we had just left. In deep sorrow we understood what it meant. We carried on walking in the direction of the ghetto wailing and mourning. That was the end of the Girul camp: all the inmates of that camp - women and children - and along with them my mother and my younger siblings - were taken to the pits in the Girul forest where they were shot and murdered.

So here is Mina's list of the fates of her nuclear family:

(Holocaust deniers, please note: Multiply this story by one million nuclear families)

THE TATTERED FAMILY OF MINA (NEE BOD) GIRSCH

My mother Rachel was murdered by gunshots together with her small children at the Girul camp (Geruliai) on 7 Elul.

Uri, born 1928, close to the age of bar mitzvah. He was shot and murdered together with my little brothers and my mother in the Girul camp.

Aharon, born 1930, was a ten-year-old in school when he was killed by gunshots in the Girul forest.

Ita, born 1932, was eight years old when she was murdered.

My father Yosef was murdered in the Rein (Rainiai) forest on 20 Elul

Moshe, born 1921, a handsome tall boy. Worked in the workshop together with father and was due to be conscripted into the army. Was murdered in the Rein forest together with my father.

Devora, my sister, born 1926, was shot to death on 5 January 1946 while attempting to emigrate to the Land of Israel

Zalman my oldest brother, born 1918, passed through the ghetto and camps. After the war he emigrated to America. Married Henia, (a relative of Haykel) whom he met in the Shavli ghetto. They had two sons: Yosi (named after my father) and Moshe (named after my brother)

Mina born, 1924, after a long path of suffering I emigrated to Israel, married Haykel and we had two daughters, Rahel and Zehava"

If that is not enough, Mina mentions more of her extended family murdered in Girul:

" . . . my aunt, my mother's sister, Gila Onia, her children and her whole family, my aunt, Haya Faivush. and many other beloved and precious members of my family, were murdered. May their memory be for a blessing. It pains me to speak about what happened to them during the days of extermination and annihilation, a sign of their pure souls. May their names and their memories be preserved in our hearts forever."

So now, in this story, we have left about 500 young Jewish women, aged 15 – 30 as the only occupants of the Telz ghetto. All the other members of their family have been slaughtered, and these mourners being used for labour (and presumably other abuse which I will not even mention).

Mina again:

In the Telz ghetto

On 7 Elul I reached the Telz Ghetto, that was situated in the poorest section of the town in the Bath House Road. The Lithuanian inhabitants left their neglected houses and went over to live in the vacant Jewish houses. The Ghetto was surrounded by a thick fence made of boards around which wire threads were stretched.

I was put into a wretched house, whose former inhabitants had emptied its contents. Because there were no beds in the house we slept on the floor. It was a ghetto consisting of 500 young girls aged between 15 and 30, who had recently lost their families. Without giving us any time to mourn our siblings and or our parents, who had just been murdered, they immediately sent us off to work in the fields.

Every day during the summer months we were sent to collect potatoes and turnips from the fields. It was hard work digging up the earth in order to extract the vegetable, after which we transferred the potatoes to the crate, and when the crate was full we lifted it up and loaded it on to the cart – they forced us to remain bent over the whole day.

I was then only 16 years old and my sister Devora was 14. With low morale and with mournful and painful hearts at the murder of our families, we continued working whilst we cried and ached. There was not a single one of us who had not lost someone in their family.

We received little food. . .

They had received news that almost all the other ghettos of small towns were liquidated as well as all Jews from small villages. It became clear that when their labour was no longer needed, they would be killed too. And this was the case. After three months in the ghetto all the girls and women there were slaughtered. But Mina and her sister made their escape just before it happened.

ESCAPE TO THE SIAULIAI GHETTO

Mina's brother, who had been in the Lithuanian army like Chaikel, and now was living in the Siauliai-Shavel ghetto with the Girsh family, organised an escape to bring Mina and her sister Devorah to them. A Lithuanian farmer with a horse-drawn wagon was arranged for them and they found an opening in the makeshift wooden fences with barbed wire wrapped around them. One night they sneaked out, dressed in "farmer's clothes", met the farmer in the designated place, and made their way to Siauliai-Shavel, arriving a few hours later. It was around Chanukah time (30 to 31 December 1941) in the middle of winter. They joined a group of Jews returning from working in the night, and entered the Ghetto, met by their brother Zalman.

Mina again:

Chaikel's parents received us pleasantly and shared the little that they had in their house with us.

In this house, that was not more than a small narrow room with a corner kitchen, lived eleven people. Four men slept in the kitchen – Haykel's father, my brother, Shmerl, Rivka's husband, and a Polish refugee. Seven people slept in the room – Haykel's mother, his two sisters, *two small grandchildren*, who often ran to sleep in their grandfather's bed, my sister and I.

And that is how it happened that Mina and her sister Devorah came to live with the Girsh family in the crowded rooms and corridors of the Siaulia-Shavel ghetto. She and Chaikel fell in love, and promised each other that if they would survive the war, they would marry, and create a future together . . .

AUNT MINA IN THE
SIAULIAI GHETTO

The first ghetto in Shavel the Germans created was named the Kaukasa (Caucasus) ghetto (perhaps because the Germans were hoping to conquer Russia and be in possession of the rich oil resources in the Caucasus). It was in a poor area of wooden hovels, with some poor Jews and some poor Christians living there. Its border was on the Jewish cemetery. Shmuel Kerbelis, an active member of the Jewish community of Siauliai, whose mother was a survivor who stayed on in Lithuania after the war, told me that in the beginning the Jewish cemetery was included in the boundary of the ghetto. In that time, a Jew dying in the ghetto could still have a half-proper burial in the cemetery there —a unique individual grave. On the side opposite the cemetery, across Vilnius road, was the Frenkel factory and villa. The Frenkel Palace is still a major tourist attraction today, with lots of art and artifacts of the land. The old factory buildings are mostly deserted, still stand there today. Two tall redbrick chimneys grace the skyline.

When the Kaukasa ghetto was getting too full, the Germans opened up a second ghetto, in the Traku quarter, just about a quarter mile from the first ghetto. It was from here that Grandma, and little Moishele and Sarele were taken on 5th November 1941.

Uncle Chaikel, being qualified in many areas to do with machining, and having excellent mechanical knowledge, was useful to the Nazis, and so he got an indoors job in one of the Frenkel Villa factories, literally across the road from the ghetto. The Girsh family home had been literally up the road from the ghetto, so that their move from their ransacked home to the ghetto, was a short one.

But the three girls, Mina and her two future sisters-in-law, Rivke and Mary, had to do hard labour work, and mainly outdoors. Mina first worked at a train yard ("Dafu") breaking up coal and transferring the pieces onto coal trucks. She was perpetually black and had almost no washing resources in the ghetto. She could not wash her clothing. A later job involved digging up peat from the earth. Then there was the work at what she called Zuknah airport.

Mina writes about how they had to march to the Zukniai airport every day, work like slaves all day, then march all the way back:

In October 1943 the Ministry of Labour requested more Jews from the ghetto to work at the airport. An order was issued that about 500 Jews were required. They would live at the airport so as not to waste time getting to work. Though Chaikel was in a good situation at the factory, he chose to apply for the airport post so that he could be near Mina, who would now be living there and not be with him in the ghetto. That way they could be supportive of each other there.

I saw on *Apple Maps* there is a "Siauliai International Airport" in the Zukniai area that uncle and aunt wrote about. On my bicycle I followed the signs to the airport. This must have been the very road that aunt Mina walked down and back from daily for a time. I measured the distance as about 3 ½ miles (5 km's plus). Nothing like a brisk march like that after a hard day's work on not-enough food to sustain one. Mina writes that all she cared about was to get home to sit down at last!!

There is no international airport there now!

I expected a small, bustling airport. Not a passenger plane in sight, on earth or in the heavens! Only military ones. An airport building for the public, for non-military flights, was an office block, which had not a single human being in it! It had closed doors one has to pass through for "customs" and "passport control". Ghostly!

I cycled a bit around the area and found an old disused landing strip made up roughly of laid concrete blocks. To each side were a number of large quonset huts with huge metal locked doors. I felt sure that aunt Mina must have been part of the work team laying that old runway, because she wrote about levelling the ground for a new runway. But I had heard worse stories about it. There had been about 100 Russian prisoners kept here which the Germans had captured in their takeover of the airport. Shmuel Kerbelis told me that these were treated even worse than the Jewish workers and were starved so drastically that they resorted to cannibalism to stay alive. Eventually they were all killed and their bodies buried under the developing runway.

MY FATHER'S
SIAULIAI-SHAVEL HOME

On the early evening that I first arrived from Vilnius by train in my father's home town, Siauliai-Shavel, and got on my bicycle to seek my cheap hotel far from the central area. I wondered what my eyes were falling on that my father, in his young life before leaving for South Africa, would also have seen. Were there old structures, old churches, which were already there from 1910? I photographed an old church near the station —The Church of Saint George, then a red-bricked water tower, and so on. I simply did not know where I was in relation to where my grandparents and their family lived. In the night I just had the strange sense that "somewhere not far from here, all the history of my father's family took place. The children all played, did sport (mainly football and ice skating), the grandparents were very industrious, both making a living, and being very charitable to the needy. From here the three sons had said goodbye, probably forever, as they emigrated to South Africa. Then later it ended with the history of those who remained in Siauliai and were caught up in the Holocaust".

The family's home address was 98 Vilnius street, Siauliai. As a young man, my father had printed up a personal "calling card" with his name and that address on it. I had found the card among his South African possessions after he died. But I also went to the city's archive offices in Siauliai central, and they confirmed that Aron Girsh had a property at 98 Vilnius gatve, and had a list of the people who lived there in 1938 (The children had left home and he obviously had some boarders there. He had built homes for the two daughters just next door).

Arriving at the address, just a little way out of the centre, I found at least 3 street numbers totally unoccupied —96 to 98 Vilnius street. All I could do is imagine, how the boys played football (a lot of enthusiasm for that in the family), how aunty Rivke became a highly skilled ice-skater, coming second in some championship competition in Siauliai. My father used to say that he skated miles down a river in winter, against the wind, and then would open up his jacket and "sailed" back again. In hot South Africa we have a serious shortage of iced-over rivers, and certainly none you could skate on. I never associated my father with ice-skating, until one day, on holiday at the seaside in Durban, at the ice rink, he put on a pair of skates and away he went with the greatest of ease on the skates. We children had no clue he could ice skate. It was a snapshot of is past that hit our eyes for a brief moment.

So . . . it all happened somewhere around here . . . all around here . . . in a world that looked very different from what it looks like today. Uncle Chaikel had written little about the specifics of the environment around them . . . or what he had written about was probably changed and gone. So it was a delight, on a Facebook group of the Jewish descendants of people from Siauliai-Shavel, that someone posted a picture of a flat field area that apparently used to be used as an ice-skating rink. Ah! That's how aunty Rivke managed to practice her sport right in town!

Well, Frenkel's factory, and the red chimneys looming over it, for sure were there during my father's youth — less than a mile down the road from where they lived. It turned out that I could do something more than just *see* something that my father and all the other family must have seen.

I could *touch* something my grandfather almost certainly touched. Re-reading my uncle and aunt's book, I had missed one sentence (as one does when one reads): it is almost certain that my grandfather *built* the first of those chimneys. There is quite bit of evidence in favour of this. He had a factory of building materials, including a manufacturing of red bricks, and he did do much masonry, brick-laying work himself. So, I went up to the bricks and laid my hands on them . . .imagining that past and present were meeting here . . . that my grandad's hands had touched the very bricks I was touching now.

On my arrival in Siauliai, by train, I had a fellow cycling co-traveller take a photo of me at the Siauliai station. I felt I was miles away from where the live action of my family had happened so many years ago, and that I would have to consult a map, and discover where I could see the places of my family's history. Then, two weeks after my journey, on the website of Jewish descendants of Siauliai Jews, someone posted a picture of the very station where I had stood for a photo, and told that it was from here, exactly from here, that the surviving Jews from the Siauliai ghetto were transported to the Stutthof concentration camp near Gdansk, in Poland, when it was clear that Germany was losing the war. Ah, even here, on arrival, I was already, unknowingly, at a spot that my uncle and aunt, my uncle's two sisters, and grandad, had all passed through, on their deportation to the Stutthof Concentration camp destined for annihilation.

Grandpa Aron Girsh was murdered there in July 1944. But the Germans were beginning to lose the war, and they were taking their victims further away from the slowly conquering Russians. From Stutthof uncle Chaikel was deported to the Dachau concentration camp outside of Munich.

UNCLE CHAIKEL IN DACHAU

Uncle Chaikel tells us:

When the work at the airport (Siauliai) was finished (May 1944) they transferred us to work at another airport near to Ponevezh, about 60 kilometres from Shavli. The living conditions at the airport near Ponevezh were much worse than in the Shavli camps - the food was poor and the discipline at work was very severe. They gave us hard labour like loading wagons with bricks and with cement.

We remained there for about two months, and after that they brought us back to the Shavli Ghetto together with Jews who were at other labour camps. The Germans concentrated everyone in the ghetto because the war front was getting closer. Up to this point, everyone who had managed to flee or to hide – was saved, because the Russians began to enter the territories that had been conquered by the Germans. Out of 3 000 Jews who had been sent to the Shavli ghetto, only about 500 managed to survive to see the day of Liberation.

We were in the ghetto for one night, and the next day they transported us in trains to Germany to the Stutthof concentration camp on the shores of the Baltic next to Danzig (July 1944). In this camp were concentrated Jews who were transferred from the Baltic countries and Poland.

When we reached Stutthof we were taken off the train and made to stand in front of a column of trees. The German police separated the men and the women, putting the women on the left side, and the men on the right side. They arranged us in rows, five people in each row. Mina – whom I never saw again after this not for several years – walked in a fivesome together with her sister Devora, my two sisters (Rivka and Miriam) and Henia (the grandchild of my uncle Leizer and the future wife of Zalman, Mina's brother). We men organised a fivesome on the other side – I marched at the side of my father, Zalman, Mina's brother, my brother-in-law, Shmaryahu (husband of my sister Rivka) and my cousin Berl.

Thus we walked until we entered the camp. There was a huge riot there, the Germans treated us cruelly and aggressively. They crammed us into a hut while hitting us with clubs. We remained the whole night crushed against each other unable to move and for sure not of leaving the hut. With all the pressure that there was at the time I never saw father again. The last time I saw him was when we entered the camp. It never occurred to us that we would never see each other again. We thought we would still meet and be able to be together again. Only the next morning they ordered us, the younger ones, to leave the camp and to get on to the trains that would take us to the Dachau concentration camp in Germany. The others – the sick, pregnant women and the elderly – and my father among them, they left there. They were taken to the hut of those who were doomed to die, they took off their clothes and their shoes, beat them and wouldn't let them move from their place even to relieve themselves. From there they were transferred to the crematorium and there they were put to death.

From Stutthof convoys went out to all the German death camps. Mothers with their children were sent to Auschwitz and there they were cremated. A small number of women who were in the labour force, were sent to Dachau, and among them were Mina and my sisters who were sent to work in the fields or were transferred to labour camps in east Prussia. They experienced terrible unspeakable things and only very few were saved.

They put us on a freight train that took us to Dachau. It was a long journey and we sat on the floor one on top of the other.

I will let uncle Chaikel tell his Dachau story in his own words. I cut out substantial parts from the book, all about various strategies, strokes of luck and so on that helped him survive.

A BRIEF HISTORY OF UNCLE CHAIKEL IN DACHAU CONCENTRATION CAMP

From Uncle Chaikel's writings:

Dachau Camp, that is located about 15 kilometres north west of Munich, was one of the first concentration camps established by the Nazis. When we got to Dachau, they told us to take off our clothes and to wash and after that they shaved us.

❖

They attached a number to each person, and they did not call us by our names – each one of us was a number.

After that they divided us into working groups and by the following day they sent all of the groups out to one of twelve labour camps that were in the vicinity.

❖

The hunger was unbearable, and against this calamity we were helpless. The hunger brought us closer to the harvest of death, and every day hundreds of people were buried. The only food we received in the camp was soup and one piece of bread, . . .

The soup was watery, one could say warm water. Sometimes a piece of potato or beetroot, fell into your soup and that was considered to be a good portion. Sometimes if you were lucky there was also a piece of cabbage

❖

At a certain stage the Germans decided to fumigate the camp because of the increase in the lice. They put us in the showers and ordered us to get undressed and to wash ourselves and they sprinkled us with liquid disinfectant. After that we were forced to wait outside naked for a couple of hours in the freezing cold until they brought us a change of clothes that had been disinfected. The cold was terrible, and we stood one against the other shivering. There were some who became ill with inflammation of the lungs as a result and died several days later, among them was my uncle Yosef.

❖

Conditions in the camp were hard, and the relationship of the Germans towards us was disgraceful. One day I was hit by a German guard, who saw me walking alone in the forest (I was apparently going to fetch something). The guard took me into the guard room and punched me with his fist. As a result I lost one of my teeth.

❖

At a certain stage they brought 800 Jews to the camp directly from their homes in Czechoslovakia. These people were still at the peak of their strength and had not yet experienced the suffering of the people in the camps. Within three months only three tenths of them remained whom they allocated to the other groups. We were all emaciated, skeletons musselmener, (a name that was given to people who had no flesh on their bones). At the time of the Liberation I weighed 44 kilos (96 lbs) and I was among the strong ones.

❖

I remained in Camp 1 about a month until they transferred me and all who remained alive back to the Central camp in Dachau. We were in Dachau for one night. That whole night they left us sitting on the field. I remember that night standing on the field in the camp, the sight of the soldiers with typhus and the wagons loaded with the dead, left an indelible impression upon me.

❖

There were also Polish criminals among the prisoners in Dachau. These prisoners organised a rebellion and towards the morning they attacked the camp stores, many Jews participated in this. In the confusion I succeeded in grabbing a pair of shoes, that was very helpful to me on the death march that began the following day.

We were in those camps for about ten months, and whoever did not have shoes, had no chance to survive and to remain alive.

❖

Death march: On 26 April 1945 they took us out of Dachau on a death march. Over 7000 Jews were forced to march south under the supervision of the SS who shot anyone who faltered along the way. After some time the Germans could hear the echo of the bombing of the Americans. And they changed the direction of the march so as to distance us from the front that was getting closer. Many of us collapsed from hunger and fatigue along the way; whoever could not walk was shot. We

---

walked from the morning to the evening almost entirely without food, and in the evening we stopped. Some people made a fire and we sat around it to get a bit of warmth. It was cold and the ground was wet, so that it was not possible to lie down or to try to get a little sleep, but only to sit on a stone or something similar.

At a certain stage my friend Shalom and myself decided to flee. I already felt that the end of the war was near and we did not know what end the Germans, who all the time had their guns pointed at us, were planning for us. We neared the right side of the road, where there was a forest with a winding slope leading to it. Evening came. At the first opportunity we lay on the ground and rolled down the length of the slope of the mountain. We remained lying down on the slope next to the trees until the whole convoy had passed. We continued to lie like this the whole night. In the morning we began to walk. We hid another night in a small hut in which we found the backpacks of German soldiers who had fled from the American army. To our delight, in the back packs we found soldier's equipment that included: vests, underpants, socks and suchlike things. Each one of us put on the clothes and the clean warm underwear, and in the morning we continued walking. We arrived at a very large village where the American army had already arrived.

Finally we were liberated.

MINA'S DEATH MARCH

Mina too had been sent, from Stutthof, on a death march.

I had a companion, who accompanied me and became a friend and walked with me all the way, his name was hunger. In the face of this calamity I was at a loss. This hunger was designed by our persecutors in order to weaken our resistance to the harvest of death. And as it is was once said "the victims of the sword are more fortunate than the victims of hunger." (Lamentations 4, 9). And the victims of hunger in those days of extermination were many in number. Days and nights for many months and years we suffered and struggled against monstrous hunger pangs, that held us in their choking grasp. It is difficult today to convey to people who are sated, who have never experienced these hunger pangs, who have never known what hunger is, the overwhelming desire for bread and the great craving for food just to feel satisfied. We dreamt that even just once, a day would come when we would be able to cut a whole loaf of bread up into pieces and eat to our heart's content with no limits

Many religious Jews began to doubt the existence of a God who allowed such a catastrophe to happen. Many others thought differently - maybe God was punishing us for our sins whatever they may be. On account of my difficult circumstances, I could not bother myself with questions of religion and God, but I focused mainly on thinking of what would happen tomorrow.

Well, that is also seriously dumb thinking —that God was punishing the Jews for their sins. This is as irrational as the German dumb thinking. It places the Germans as instruments of God, and eliminates the commandment that "Thou shalt not kill", justifies killing, suggests that a whole nation, generalised, can be more sinful than any other whole nation, which means that even if you are just one innocent person among a million, you are guilty by association, and it exonerates the Germans from guilt, etc. etc. It's the dumbest theological argument I have ever heard!!! It does show how easily humans are capable of feeling guilty — a psychological fact that has powerfully enabled the spreading of Christianity as the religion which rescues us from this universal "original sin". It's primitive thinking!!!

Mina again:

Death march

In January 1945 the great attack of the Red Army on Poland began. Warsaw was liberated. The cities of Krakau, Czenstochov and Lodz were also liberated. The Red Army soldiers crossed the river Oder, and for the first time walked on German land. The Auschwitz camp was evacuated, and its prisoners were taken out on a "Death march." The evacuation of the Stutthof prisoners also began.

We didn't know what we were facing. The Germans wanted to distance us from the front so that we would remain in their hands. The sick and the weak in our camp, who were not able to march, remained in the camp - among them my friend Inga – and we went on our way. My sister, Devora, walked by my side. We feared for the fate of our friends who were left behind in the camp and considered them to be wretched as their lives were at stake.

It was winter with snow and heavy frost. Wearing only light prisoner's clothes, every day we tramped through deep snow from the morning until darkness. We were worn out from hunger and from the frost. We walked and we walked. Our wooden shoes clattered on the frozen earth as we plodded along in an endless line. The SS guards who accompanied us hit us with the butt of their guns, with batons and whips and hurried the weak and the slow with kicks and blows. Whoever stumbled and fell because their strength was spent, was shot and killed on the spot. There were also women of forty and over who had difficulty walking at the same pace as the young ones. The guard who walked behind us was shooting at the stumblers all the time. More than once we heard the German guard approach the officer who walked at the head of the march and ask him to give him more bullets because he had run out.

. . .

The shoes that we wore were those that we had worn in the camp, and they were obviously unsuited to a march such as this. Often the shoes were missing a shoelace or a sole. My sister-in-law, Mary, who walked next to me complained about the pains in her legs from the cold and the difficult march. Secretly so that the guard should not see we took some snow to rub on her aching legs.

I, Aron, guess anything meant to soothe or help life, help survival, was considered a great evil by the Nazis.

The rows became fewer and fewer, and we continued to walk endlessly with no end in sight.

We passed the nights on the floor in barns, in stables, in abandoned houses and in yards without roofs. There were those who managed to flee because the policemen could not keep count of our exact numbers. On one of these days when it was already dark, they put us into a place that was filled with all sorts of foodstuffs in jars and in boxes of preserves all around it. We were starving. Nonetheless we were too frightened to eat in case the food had been poisoned.

.

The next morning we got up and saw that we were the only group left there. Apparently we had not heard everyone leaving. We went outside and we couldn't see a soul. Instead of exploiting the opportunity to escape, we began searching for the convoy. We detected some German soldiers and asked them if they had seen a big group of prisoners. The soldiers pointed us in the direction in which the group had gone. And we in our innocence began to run to join them.

.

And behold at last the long awaited and yearned for day arrived. It happened on 10 March 1945. We reached a small town, called Hinuv.

We were free! Before long we began to try to get back up on to our feet. Those who were unable to stand, tried to get up and immediately collapsed.

There were about a thousand women at the beginning of the march of whom only about a third survived and had the good fortune to be liberated.

MY POST-WAR POST-HOLOCAUST RANT

Well, having given you, dear reader, enough of those horrors of history, and the amount and scope of them from WWII is enough to keep us going with atrociousness and misery for at least a 100 years, I want to share some of my ponderings about the stupidities and contradictions and blindspots of those terrible times. And to raise what I think are some important questions!

I call it my post-war, post-Holocaust rant!

PART TWO

MY ANTI-WAR

POST-HOLOCAUST

RANT

SCIENTIFIC PSYCHOLOGY'S ATTEMPT AT UNDERSTANDING GENOCIDES

Modern neuroscience and evolutionary biology have told us something about what they call our "hard wiring" — that humans have an enormous capacity for cooperation and altruism, and that is this that enabled humans to survive among animals which were much faster and stronger than they. Well this is all very well, but how do we explain human lack of cooperation, human conflict and destructiveness, since time immemorial.

There are at least four well-known experiments undertaken by university psychology faculties trying to understand some of this human psychology which predisposes humans to such amazing destructiveness.

Perhaps the most famous is the Milgram experiment, done by Stanley Milgram, at Yale University in 1961, just after the trial of Adolf Eichmann, one of the main Nazi criminals. Nazi war criminals being tried at the Nuremburg courts argued that they were just following orders, just "being obedient". The experiment is described as an experiment to test obedience to authority versus personal conscience. It tested to see how far a person would go to electrically shock another person unseen in an adjoining room even though the person might be screaming from pain and/or being asked to be let out. The unseen person was not actually getting shocked, but was an actor performing as if he was (men only in this experiment). The generator with switch showed voltages from a low, benign 15-volt shock to a fatally dangerous 450 volts. It was found that the presence of an authority figure in a lab coat basically giving the okay for the subject to keep shocking, at higher and higher levels, the unseen person, resulted in about 65 % of the subjects going all the way to the maximum shock level — registered on the indicator as highly dangerous. All the participants went as far as the very painful 300 volts.

Another famous experiment was the Asch experiment on conformity, by Solomon Asch in the 1950's. A group, sitting in a circle, secretly part of the experiment, would evaluate some fact, shown on a blackboard, in the most distorted way. There was a go-around in the group stating what they saw, and the subject of the experiment, the person being studied, who did not know it was a setup, was the last in the circle to comment. Though the answer

---

was clearly Y, all in the group claimed they saw that it as X. So when it came to the subject's turn, would he say X or would he say Y, to conform, and to deny the reality of his own senses? Subjects do this to "fit in".

It was especially hard for the subject to resist conformity and trust his own senses when the group was unanimous in giving a false reading of reality. Over various forms of the experiment, they found roughly between 1/3 and 2/3rds of people conformed. But what was interesting was that when only one other in the group resisted the group before the subject's call, very few subjects conformed. Well, there is some encouragement to you to stick your neck out when it is important, and hopefully not too dangerous, to do so, and to fight for . . . well, either for truth, in situations where truth can be established if there is a will to do so, or to fight for love, when hatred and aggression is seen as the only valid action in any potentially flammable situation.

The answers, to the question afterward, "Why did you give the wrong answer" were dead interesting: some said they genuinely believed they were wrong and the group was right. Others said they knew they were right and the group was wrong but did not want to appear "peculiar" or "different". They wanted to fit in. (See the website *Simply Psychology* for neat summaries of these experiments).

(As I write this, with the BBC World Service on my radio, an Al Salvadori priest who was an ex-gang member who wanted to "fit in", confessed:

> "I was a hit man. I killed a lot of people. Because that's what was expected of me. I wanted to feel accepted")

In the Asch experiment, the fact was indeed a fact, easily verifiable with a tape measure. But in genocides, the perceptions of others are not based on verifiable facts at all. They are based on attitudes!

It is a fact that the psychological process called "projection", which shows us that often what we see in others is actually "put on them" (projected) from within ourselves. And it is a fact that projection works best when the thing or person perceived is not an easily observed fact, is an ambiguous stimulus. But human stupidity fails to see its own projections, its own constructions of the world.

This is especially so when one group sees another group as "disgusting", or "evil" or "threatening to us". The other group is then called things like "cockroaches" (Ruanda), "untermenschen" (the Nazis), "infidels" (religious wars on other religions), "uncivilised" (the slave industry), "bourgeoisie" (Communists), etc. etc. All these labels are slapped onto very ordinary, very good human citizens of the planet, who are neither evil, infidels, disgusting, uncivilised, etc. "but thinking makes it so" (as Shakespeare said in *Hamlet*).

False science, not only vague inaccurate perceptions thought to be "clear visions", can also enhance this primitive hate process. Hitler and the Germans had absolutely limited ideas of Darwin's theory of evolution, and what its implications were for human beings. They probably also did not know that Darwin said that the highest quality of human beings is Kindness. Darwin certainly did not say one human tribe should try and wipe out the others and the winner takes all! Nor that one tribe or group or collection should deliberately try and wipe out another because they deemed the other inferior! From where I sit with my highly limited knowledge of evolution, it seems as if almost all "aggression" in the animal world, is not a "going and out and conquering" but a genuine defensiveness of one's own territory and resources. Certainly animals do not go out to reek genocide on a competing tribe! And even if they did, that would not be a justification for humans to do the same!

(See Professor Andrew Marr's 3-part TV series entitled *Darwin's Dangerous Idea,* which shows how the theory of evolution took on a life of its own way beyond the world of science. That is to say, in so many places it took on meanings that went way beyond what it really meant and intended).

But both the above experiments have at least one flaw, a fatal one as I see it, in trying to create an experimental analogy to the real life Fascism of German and the Soviet Communism (the communists did not call themselves fascists, because that was "them", the Nazis, not "us", but they were equally if not more fascistic in their behaviour). In both those experiments, there was not joy or comfort or relief of those who obeyed, those who conformed. Those who obeyed in the Milgram experiment felt really bad about hurting the learning subject they were shocking, And many of those who conformed in the Asch experiment felt a sense of unease (cognitive dissonance) between what they thought the saw, and what 'society' suggested to them was reality.

In the real life situations of genocides, normal folk already have prejudices inside them not acted upon that are on the same page as the prejudices that inspire the great charismatic asshole leaders to act upon those prejudices and start destroying the lives of other people and revelling in their successes at doing it. It is false to explain the destructive behaviour of humans simply on the basis of obedience to orders —the defence of many Nazis on trial after the war. Hypothetically, we needed to establish "but did you think those orders were 'good'?" And secondly (very hypothetical): "Did you feel good being part of that system of human destruction? Did you delight in the system?" That is to say, there was no disparity between "personal conscience" and what they were "obeying" and "conforming to".

Eichmann, the guy who was tried in 1961 in an Israeli court of law (a court that assumed innocence until guilt proven) for his part in so efficiently organising the transport of Jews to Auschwitz etc., is said to have stated in court something like "I was being obedient, obeying orders well. Is that not a good thing?".

No! Dumb Asshole! My God!

It's not good to be loyal to abject evil!

As long as human beings only celebrate and love their victories (even if over real evil, like the Nazis) and fail to be sad about and grieve over the fact that conflicts had to be resolved in this way, we will forever perpetuate a culture of war. It's not that humans should not "fight" each other, compete for systems of governance which they think is the best way, but the fights have to be done without violence, and with respect for each other's different ideas as to how things should be. The competition should be: let's see who can create the most attractive system, so that people will spontaneously want to join it. After all, many flee dictatorships, emigrate to free democracies. There are very few who secretly wish, I imagine, "I must get away from this free country. This democracy is getting me down". Oh, there are a handful of radicals who think this way, but the numbers one way from dictator countries to free countries versus the numbers of the free-living desiring madly to go and live under dictatorships, must be, I would guess, about a million to one.

One other experiment attempting to figure out something about human cruelty was depicted in a movie called "The Experiment". Subjects volunteered for a two-week paid experiment where half of them would be randomly chosen to be "wardens" on a prison, and the other half "prisoners". The choices were made by the spin of a coin. The "wardens" became so cruel to the "prisoners" after a few days, that the experiment had to be stopped. Here it seems, if one reads all the details, and the later critique of the experiment, that the wardens were kind of prompted about what they could do/should to. So it becomes somewhat of a riddle as to whether they were just being cruel to conform, and whether they would have thought up those "atrocities" themselves.

At any rate, two things are notable: subjects were divided randomly, so there was no pre-selection of "cruel people" on one side, and "victim mentalities" on the other. Ostensibly, the same cruel behaviour could be evoked in all subjects, suggesting all normal people like us are vulnerable to such behaviour. But the second notable thing is that this cruel behaviour seems to have been enjoyed — unlike in the Milgram experiment.

There was another experiment conducted with young children. They were randomly divided into two imaginary groups, designated A and B. The "teacher" would then give descriptions about the "superior" characteristics of group A and the "inferior" characteristics of group B. This caused a variety of cruel communication from A to B. But then the teacher carried on with the story, adding other qualities and reversing the order of superiority/inferiority. And the cruelty flowed the other way.

THE ENEMY
—"EVIL, DISGUSTING, SUB-HUMAN, AND A THREAT TO US"

Whatever limitations these experiments might have, they do suggest the easy psychological process in human beings where we can designate others as "evil, disgusting, inhuman, and a threat to us" and convince people on our side that this is so. In the Ruandan genocide of 1994, carried out person-to-person, usually with machetes or hoes, the radio bleated out that ethnic Tutsis were "cockroaches", and they should be stamped out as such by the Hutus. It became a human-to-"Cockroach" massacre.

This is simply another example of the easy primitive binary distinction made by human nature which divides us up into "us" and "them" with "us = good, superior, clean, moral"

and

"them = bad, inferior, dirty, immoral"

Clemantine Wamariya, a Ruandan survivor, who was reunited with her family on the Oprah show, tells us in a public talk that husbands killed wives, wives killed husbands, and neighbours who had previously loved each other killed each other.

What is interesting, but sad to see, is what has often happened when there is inter-mixing between the "aryans" and the "inferior subhumans" — say a couple falling in love and marrying. For instance, in the Ruandan genocide, four years before it happened, there was already much suspicion between the two groups. But, of course, where people were open to each other, there were some mixed marriages, people falling in love. But a publication in Kangura, Ruanda, in 1990, entitled "The Ten Commandments of the Hutu) suggested the following (I have left out some of Ten):

1.   The Tutsi are blood-and-power thirsty. They want to impose their hegemony on the Rwandan people by cannon and sword. (Note how "the Rwandan people" do not include the Tutsis — who were part of the Rwandan people!)

---

2.   Tutsis tried to marry their wives to the Hutu elite in order to have spies in the inner circle.

6. Hutus must know that the Tutsi wife, wherever she may be, is serving the Tutsi ethnic group. In consequence any Hutu that does the following is a traitor:

    a) Acquires a Tutsi wife;

    b) Acquires a Tutsi concubine;

    c) Acquires a Tutsi secretary protégé

9. No military man may marry a Tutsi woman.

10. The Hutu must stop taking pity on the Tutsi.

So not only are the Tutsis inherently evil and a threat, but their women are being used to infiltrate and spy on the Hutus by "pretending" to fall in love with a Hutu. Wow!

When the genocide began the radio communique broadcast endlessly about the evils of the Tutsi "cockroaches". There are stories of husbands and wives turning against each other, even murdering one the other.

At a conference on the Ruanda genocide, at the Jewish Holocaust Centre in Cape Town in 1999 attended by some of the top people in the new Ruanda, we were told that the slightest hint of having genes from the "them-bad" side would automatically (read "irrationally") get a person tagged as "due for slaughter".

What is really revealing of the human stupidity is what happens when a mixed-race/mixed-tribe child has been born, in this case, half Hutu, half Tutsi. We were told stories like this:

A Hutu father, a Tutsi mother produce a mixed-race child whom they love. But one day Hutus are told that Tutsis are bad and the cause of all the problems for the Hutus, and the child got an "evil" tag (as a "cockroach") on it and thus was slaughtered by its own father. Apparently this sort of thing happened a lot in the Ruandan genocide.

The *child* got labelled as *evil* (and therefore guilty) *by his own father!!!*

Not even a hint of "Mmmh! This child is half good and half bad. So what decision should I make about it. Mmmmh! Difficult decision" I am being ironic, of course!

In Apartheid South Africa, where I grew up, I often heard the following said by whites about the "Coloureds" —the mixed race folk who do not speak any African language, but speak the language of the White Afrikaners: "They combine the worst qualities of black and white!".

Wow! Even in this highly prejudiced statement there is at least the implicit acknowledgment that there is indeed badness even in the white race. But I never heard the opposite view, which has more truth: The Coloureds, mixed race folk of South Africa combine *the best qualities* of both races.

Of course, all this is very simplistic, over-simplistic thinking about race and intelligence and human qualities. I am simply pointing out the dumb irrationality even within those dumb, limited narratives.

In Germany there had been a lot of "inter-breeding" anyway between Jews and Christians. But the Nazis decided that anyone with 1/8 th Jewish blood was designated as a Jew (there were those who wanted the definition to be extended to $1/16^{th}$).

Gosh! Such clear thinking (ironic). If a person contains 7/8 Aryanism, surely we should have mixed feelings about what to do with him or her. I mean . . 7/8th pure Aryan goodness, truth and beauty . . . and only $1/8^{th}$ Jewish badness, lying and ugliness. . .

Ah, I guess the smallest germ or virus in a body can wreak terrible devastation! We need good hygiene!

THE USELESSNESS OF WAR

This human psychology that we are "it" and they are "them" and therefore "a threat to us" and therefore "the enemy" seems to be a stronger force motivating people to war than the inevitably impoverishing consequences of war. Believe it or not, even before WWI someone had worked out that war was useless, profited no one.

Margaret MacMillan, the 2018 Reith Lecturer for the BBC's series "The Mark of Cain" tells us:

"There was a fascinating man called Ivan Bloch, a Polish Jew, who had moved to Russia before the first WW and made a fortune in financing. He had built many of the Russian railways, and, worried about the state of the world, like Alfred Nobel, he turned his considerable fortune, and considerable intellect, to looking at war, and he wrote a massive 6-volume book on the future of war and in it he said:

'the European powers now have the capacity to fight wars on a very large scale for a very long time. . . and what they will do is end up with a stalemate, because, both sides are so equally balanced that no side can defeat the other. Each side can hold the other off, prevent victory'.

He foresaw very clearly what was going to happen in the first world war, he predicted it, and, by and large, he was absolutely right.

He believed that if he pointed this out to people, that if he kept telling people that he was running the risk of such a war, that they were going to destroy themselves and their own societies if they got into a conflict which could not be resolved easily, that they could get into a conflict that would last for years. He believed that if he told people this, and they would believe him.

'There will be no war in the future', he told his British publisher, 'for it has become impossible, now that it is clear that war means suicide'"

But human primitive psychology, unable to clearly think of the consequences of their actions, managed to create a very fine war, "the war to end all wars". This seems to be a big part of human psychology — "By means of this last, final, war, of good against evil, we will at last achieve peace". All the so-called "reasons for war" are really "excuses for war" and generally there is a primitive human psychology working itself out. And all the so-called "Causes of a war" suggest that there are some kinds of impersonal "causes" with determinably cause "effects", in this case fighting and violence, as if humans have no choice when a certain "cause" causes a certain "effect". Actually, that listed cause was not really *the cause* of war! It was *the reason* chosen as an excuse to go to war. We refused to try other methods to resolve the conflict, even though we had incredible resources to do so, but we chose to spend those resources on mega-expensive weapons and on human devastation. For God's sake, are we humans going to continue to talk about ourselves as if we are robots who, when a button is pressed, has no choice in their reactions!!! We hear this kind of talk in relation to population explosion. "Population *will* increase by X% in the next 30 years". We have no choice??? Can we not choose to decrease population by X% in the next 30 years??? Robots or humans. Choose!!!

HOW HUMANS ARE PREDISPOSED TO WAR

Though it is slightly more complex than this, the following is the most important underlying process in human nature that predisposes us so easily to war.

There is an easy ability in humans to see outsiders as either evil, disgusting, inhuman (untermenschen), or "a threat to us" David Irving, the right wing apologist historian for the Germans, anti-hero in the movie "Denial", about the Holocaust, argued in his 1977 book, *Hitler's War*, that the German invasion of the Soviet Union in 1941 was a 'preventative war' forced on Hitler to prevent an impending Soviet attack. Poor victimised Hitler! And, to the best of my highly limited knowledge, every one of the combatants in WWI described their war as a defensive war. Perhaps, over the last few hundred years or so in Europe, since the Peace of Westphalia in 1648, it became slightly less okay to say "We are going to fight an aggressive war, conquering war with you other Europeans", so the excuse "you are getting dangerous and we have to be sure we can defend ourselves —so we might have to attack you" became more fashionable.

So this is the psychology of war: Humans have inside us the easily ability to perceive 'them' as all those bad things and a threat —even if and when they are not . But it is generally a totally false perception. We are simply projecting a false image onto "them".

Am I saying there is no real threat from "the other"?

<u>I am not!!!</u>

The above is the default "insides" of human beings. Our psyches are "idling", like a stationary car, with that, ready to take off at high acceleration with all that power waiting to be used. But every now and then one side *decides to act* on their false perceptions and attack! The other side now can see very clearly that the first side is *really* a threat —*because it is really a threat!.* So now they have to attack back . . . for defence! And have to defend —to attack back. And so the human spiral of violence is one of the easies electrical circuit boards to light up.

War is a guaranteed self-fulfilling prophecy because it is always an ambiguous stimulus we are looking at when we look at the other side — we really don't know their true intentions because they themselves don't know their true intentions because what they intend to do depends on what we intend to do and they can't be sure exactly what we intend to do because we ourselves are not sure what we intend to do. And, as psychology teaches us, when there is an ambiguous, vague stimulus (like in the Rorschach inkblots) humans easily project their own imaginations onto it, putting things onto the picture that are really not a part of the actual picture.

And, because primitive human nature predisposes us so easily to see threat from the other side, it means we are always facing each other as potentially threatening. And as soon as one side chooses "to attack to defend" the previously ambiguous threat easily becomes a real threat, and real evil and destruction festers.

This means it really is difficult for one side to choose peace and/or non-violence if the other side won't do the same. The Nazis had to be stopped. There was nothing else to do. I cannot choose peace if you refuse to do so and insist on attacking.

That is basically the psychology of war, which has killed zillions of very fine human folk on the planet. It's a pretty dumb, unthought-out human process, primitive psychology. But it is as I said in the opening lines to this book, very human! If we cannot solve this psychological problem, we will never solve the problem of war. Humans will somehow discover themselves creating it over and over and over and over again, as they have since the organisation of societies began.

Interesting that Bloch said war can only end in suicide. Hitler and Eva Braun, Joseph Goebbels and his wife and 6 children all ended the Nazi time by committing suicide. But they had not just committed suicide themselves. The whole German nation had committed suicide by their stupid aggressiveness and dumb ideologies.

By committing murder, they had committed suicide!

But, for the current situation of incredibly low emotional and spiritual intelligence on the planet, the best we can do is see to it that we are not the perpetrators, be very clear about our commitment to non-violence, very clear about our morality in this — that we shall do all we can to reduce the killing.

Ivan Bloch, the Jew I mentioned who tried to persuade the world that war was useless economically, does seem to have had an implicit principle favouring militarisation anyway —that nations won't attack each other, and the destruction would be two-sided and futile, *provided there was a balance of power.* So it *is* understandable where the citizens of planet earth have come to at this point in history —making sure we keep up a balance of power. But, my God! We have a long way to go to achieve a non-violent planet — and we need to wake up to this and start moving in that direction. This book is one of a million others trying to encourage the world to do that!

For a start, we can commit to definitely not being perpetrators of violence. And, even if we really have to fight really defensive wars, we can at least try to dissuade those who choose to act on their lowest instincts from doing so. We can, and should, as a nation (whichever nation) stand up and state openly that we are committed to moving towards a future of a world without war (www). And we can challenge and invite others to do the same. I know! I know! It won't work! Because humans are greedy, etc. etc. But let's make a start. Let's at least get to the starting line of that process. If you do not get to the starting line of a race you have zero chance of winning it. Perhaps one day, instead of an Arms Race, we can have a Peace Race.

Speaking of Peace Races, or at least of Peace Rides . .

There is a delightful museum of the bicycle in Vilnius street, Siauliai, not far from the centre and not far from where my grandpa, Aron Girsh lived with his family. Here there is information on "The Great Millennium Peace Ride" around the world. Organised by 47-year old Lithuanian Sigitas Kucas, a physicist by profession, it involved 10 Lithuanian cyclists, supported by Unesco, but basically paying for themselves, to cycle about 25,000 kilometres from Seattle, Washington state, USA to Hiroshima in Japan, site of the first atomic bomb used in war. They left on 6th August 1998 and arrived in Hiroshima 1st January 2000. It was a ride to promote peace and ecology. Its symbolic task was to invite people to live in peace in the new millennium and to promote the bicycle as the healthiest and most environmentally friendly means of transportation. Only 4 of the Lithuanians managed to finish the ride. They visited 45 countries in 5 continents: Northern and Southern America, Africa, Europe and Asia. Lithuania was 27th on the list.

Sigitas Kucas bicycle, with all its panniers as it was packed, is on display in the museum.

I sometimes wonder if the Americans could not simply have informed the Japanese of the terrible power they now had in their hands, shown them a movie of the first atomic explosion at Los Alamos, and warned them that if they do not surrender and stop their destructive aggressive ways, they were going to get this bomb. Might that have prevented the sufferings of so many charcoaled, seared, blackened, cancered innocent civilians.

I often in life have heard tough people sprout the idea that "there are no innocent bystanders!". Do you mean that every bystander is guilty of the crime they are in close proximity to? Wow! You mean if you witnessed something terrible happening that you would be responsible for that atrocity? That's a very quick way to designate someone as "guilty". Perhaps you need to think a bit further and differentiate *guilt as a perpetrator* from *responsibility as a witness.*

RUSSIAN MEMORIALS
IN LITHUANIA
AFTER THE WAR

The Russians, after the war, in the territories controlled by them, made a point about not remembering and honouring Russian Jews who had died in the Holocaust, and who were the majority innocent victims, but instead insisted on memorials that remembered "Soviet Citizens". In doing that, with one fell swoop, they wiped out the identity of the Jewish people, placing being Jewish into a blind spot, wiping out Jewish identity in the Soviet mind. To me it is like the burning of the books, in Berlin in 1933. A Jewish writer, years before in 1823, Heinrich Heine, came up with a now-famous quote

"Where books are burnt, people will be burnt in the end"

("Dort wo man Bücher verbrennt, verbrennt man auch am Ende Menschen,")

Well, where identity is wiped out this way, people will be wiped out in the end. And indeed, the communists were certainly ready to wipe out almost anybody with any religion, because religion, considered to be "the opiate of the people", was considered evil, because opiates are drugs that sooth and therefore stupefy, and believing in fascist communism was considered to be "anti-opiate", motivating one to take up the struggle, and, as opposed to "stupefying", would "intelligent-fy" . . . wake us up to the great, amazing, all-knowing, final solution to the human problem — Soviet communism! Now, in 2019, the Chinese, the BBC World Service tells us, are doing this to the Muslims in China by a program of forced "re-education" — so that these "unenlightened" Muslims can learn "the truth" about the good life and the nature of society and the universe.

It's part of a dangerous wiring circuit in the brain which says: "If you are not with us, you are against us". Seems to me this is a universal primitive (and therefore stupid) human psychology, probably responsible for almost every war, genocide, mass-murder, etc. etc.

Because! No!

Actually our higher brain, if we could, if we would use it, knows that this idea is absolutely crappy and dumb!!!

If I am not with you, it does not mean I am against you!!!

It means I am with myself!!!

And my existence, if I am not trying to change you, force you, threaten you, is not a threat to you —if only you can be with yourself . . . and not try to change me, force me, threaten me . . . as if the path I have chosen is inherently taking something away from you.

Well, if there is one thing I think we have to grant to the Jews. They kept to themselves as a distinct identity within all the other countries that the Roman invasion of old Israel/Palestine dispersed them to, but to the best of my highly limited knowledge, never had intentions of becoming a population majority anywhere and take over the governance of any host country. There was always, it seems, this respect for their hosts, that they were guests, no matter what.

I get the idea that this was clearly true in Lithuania. The numbers of Jews in some towns made them the majority, in many they were a large percentage of the town's population. But there was no talk of taking over the governance of town or whole country to the best of my knowledge.

Seems there are other minority groups these days that have elements in them that talk, secretly or openly, about taking over the governance of their host country, and controlling according to their rules, their ways, their limiting traditions. This is one force in right-wing backlash.

JEWISH CONSPIRACY THEORIES

The Haters of Jews often come up with all kinds of conspiracy theories. The main one is that there is a Jewish conspiracy to rule the world. Another one is that world is manipulated by powerful Jewish bankers.

My God! Neither myself, nor any other Jew I know, many of whom have been involved in all kinds of Jewish organisations, have ever been approached by any "Big Brother" and been told "Son, (or Daughter), you are aware we are working towards taking over the world. Here is how you can play your part. These are the secrets you must swear to keep for the sake of our nation"

My God! If that ever happens . . . there are so many varieties of Jews with so many different philosophies, beliefs, ideologies, that someone from the Jewish community would have exposed that one two three. It is just such absolute crap! Jewish atheists argue openly against religious Jews. Socialistic Jews argue openly against Capitalistic Jews. Pro-Palestinian Jews argue openly with anti-Palestinian Jews. Jews who believe in a single-state solution in Israel/Palestine argue with Jews who believe in a 2-state solution! Any Jew approached secretly by any Jewish conspirators would expose them instantly. And it would be safe to do so.

The same applies to the world being ruled by Jewish bankers. Whenever, in any Jewish organisation, there are people chosen to represent Jewish interests, *they are not bankers!!!* So I don't know if there are some evil Jewish bankers . . . if there are I will be glad to confront them, but I do know this: they are not representatives of the Jewish nation! *"Not in my Jewish name"* do they act. And apart from that fact, there are a host of other non-Jewish powerful bankers in the world, Protestants, Catholics, Muslims, Hindus and so on — why are they not equally picked on? Are they more moral, less immoral than the evil Jewish bankers???

I find it amazing that Jews, who did not have arms and weaponry for 2000 years now till the state of Israel was declared, who faced restrictions on land ownership, and what and where they could trade, etc., are seen as having now, and always have had, even in their most oppressed days, so much conspiratorial power. And the accusers seem oblivious to the atrocities and devastation caused by those who did in fact have armies and weaponry and power and permissions and means to destroy, and who have been responsible for the hundreds and hundreds of wars that occurred, in Europe alone, in those last 2000 years.

THE SUFFERINGS OF THE LITHUANIANS UNDER THE RUSSIANS IN THE POST-WAR YEARS

I was not unaware, in Lithuania, that the non-Jewish Lithuanians too had undergone terrible victimisation, by the Nazis in some cases, but especially by the Russians, who, after WWII incorporated Lithuania into the USSR (United Soviet Socialist Republic) because they had "liberated" it from the Nazis.

In Vilnius the building that the KGB occupied and functioned from after WWII is now a museum highlighting the atrocities of the KGB (The Russian Commission for State Security — which managed to make most of the population feel infinitely *insecure*!). There I learned that at least 100,000 Lithuanians, especially those dedicated to a free Lithuania, were sent to labour camps in Siberia. Those deportees must have been very naughty people!

And if there is anything that contributed to me calling the human race "stupid" it was my asking a few non-Jewish Lithuanian young folk if their parents or grandparents had been abused by the Russians. Every single one I asked replied in the affirmative. One though said that his grandpa and grandma managed to jump off the train to Siberia and escape and make their way back to their hometown in Lithuania. Why were they sent there? The reply was roughly this: "Oh, you must understand that anybody who had a little more than the very poor, or were very educated, professional people, were prone to be carted away".

Wow! The terrible crime of "having a bit more than others" or "being educated"!

Another story I heard was that one member of a family had written a satirical poem mocking Stalin. For this, not only he, but his immediate family and some extended family were all sent to labour camps for years. Guilt by association! There are no innocent bystanders!

One story was about a Jewish guy who wanted to marry his beloved girl and wrote a letter from Lithuania to her father in Russian. Her Jewish father was a committed communist. The young suitor had said in the letter that he was anti-Stalin. The prospective father-in-law, dumb Jew, betrayed him, reported him, out of loyalty to the cause, and he was carted off for many years to the snowy labour gulags. Loyalty is only a good thing when it is loyalty to a worthy, good cause!

The best one I heard was about a young man, a loyal communist, totally pro-Stalin, who was sitting in an inn and eating a fish. Next to him was a large picture of the egotistical, paranoid, narcissistical leader they all so admired (these portraits were everywhere, as was the case with Hitler as well). Well, out of love for the great leader, and the great communistic cause, he lifted up the fish he was eating, and offered it, "Comrade Stalin! Join me for piece of fish".

Such undignified behaviour!

He was seen and reported on and was carted off to Siberia for many years for this terrible crime!!

Dangerous Dumb human beings cause endless suffering to millions on the planet, endlessly —for the pettiest of reasons!

CONFRONTING THE DESCENDENTS

Whenever I meet an African immigrant in my native South Africa who fled from the 1994 genocide in Ruanda, I ask them if they had family killed there. One Charles said only he and his brother were left from about 26 family members killed.

Probably the biggest genocide that has ever happened in the world is the slave trade. And, for instance, in the Congo, which used to be called the Belgian Congo, King Leopold of Belgium inflicted the most abject horrors on the slaves of the rubber plantations there, which were supplying the world with a large proportion of the rubber for the tyres that rolled our vehicles, including all those war machines, to their further destruction. Actually, like the top Nazis, some of whom could not face the horrors of the killing fields, Leopold seems to have simply nodded his approval, to his lackeys, of the direst measures to control the black slave population.

One could go on and on . . .

The point I am making is that if and whenever I meet folk from any genocidal or war regions, I ask them if they had family who had perished there. So I have often wondered in my life why non-Jews, when they learn that I am Jewish, do not ask: "Did you have family in Europe who were killed in the Holocaust?"

Dear non-Jewish friends!

Do you think the Holocaust happened to some abstract group of Jews from the planet mars?

No!!!

 it happened to us!

To our families!

We, the living, living among you!

I hope this book makes you aware of this!

In relation to all nations and people who have experienced such large-scale atrocities!

But as I write this, I notice that it's easy for me to ask, to confront the pain of *the descendants of the victims* of all this primitive human stupidity. "Did you have family who died or suffered in . . . .???"

Asking about the possibility of *the guilt of your ancestors* in *perpetrating the atrocities* is somehow harder, more complex.

Because, asking a German person now "Was your father or grandfather a staunch antisemitic Nazi in the war" feels very accusing.

Because, it is not only common sense, but I believe it is written into the religions, that a child is born totally innocent of the sins of the parents and grandparents. Accusing a child of being part of a system where its grandparents killed your grandparents is seriously dumb behaviour. And yet, it happens countless times on this planet of ours.

One of the dumbest notions is the widespread Christian notion that "The Jews killed Christ". Me personally, I did not kill Christ. I was born 1945 years after him and was not around at the time. Not only that, but I would not have validated his killing, being a believer in free speech. I would have realised that the Roman emperors, great regressed narcissists many of them, would have been threatened by someone calling himself a "king". It was actually Pontius Pilate, under the Roman Emperor Tiberias, who gave the order for Jesus's crucifixion. Why did no one, over the years, attack Romans, and cry "The Romans killed Christ!"?

May I suggest that if you are one of these Christians dumb enough to have this belief, that you deal with the countless atrocities that the Christians, over 2000 years, have meted out on so many innocents. Forgive me, my dear Christian friends, you who are not so dumb, for this particular rant. The Crusades were not really what any true God would have wanted!

Haters! Look inside yourselves for the source of your hatred!

I realised at last why asking the question as to "Whether your grandfather was a perpetrator" is a hard one. Because, I think, there is a subtle accusation there, an unconscious one that most of us don't realise.

The accusation is this: Okay, so you are totally innocent. But what I am accusing you of is trying to forget, to deny your grandfather's past. Of course you are one hundred percent innocent of the atrocities! But please don't be guilty of not acknowledging your grandfather's role in them . . . or your nation's role in them!

But even to do that is to accuse the person of coming from a group that inherently has some sort of bestial flaw in it, a flaw that is unique to that group, and not to the whole of humanity.

Well, that's a false accusation too!

I grew up in an environment that considered that all Germans inherently contained the seed of evil. Who can blame us! It did not matter if we met a German who seemed a perfectly nice, compassionate person. Inside them, the seed of evil was waiting to be sprouted at any moment.

It seems as if this might have been quite a wide-spread perception for a while. An article by S.A. McLeod, in October 2007, in Simply Psychology, in which he discusses the Milgram experiment, suggests:

"Stanley Milgram set out to test the research question 'are Germans different?', but he quickly found that we are all surprisingly obedient to people in authority."

It took a while for me to correct this view of mine of the Germans. Over my wild well-spent youth I fell in love with one or two German women. One of these

---

relationships "produced" a beautiful, highly intelligent god-child for me. I met her mother at a week-long workshop in Berlin entitled "Essential Peacemaking", run by Danaan Parry, author of Warrior of the Heart". He was a big-hearted huggy-bear of a man who had, around the world, got conflicting parties, in war situations, to talk to each other, Protestants and Catholics in Northern Ireland, Israelis and Palestinians, Americans and North Vietnamese, etc. I was in love, and we spent a lot of time together, but she had a boyfriend back home, whom married soon after. But I was chosen to be the godfather of their child.

Travelling to Germany I met her family, and discovered that her sister, a medical doctor, played violin in a musical band of Germans who played Klezmer music, sang Klezmer songs — the folk tradition songs of the Jews of Eastern Europe, a whole, long tradition. I was invited to visit the sister down in the Black Forest, South Germany near the Rhine, where one night I was sitting in a German home listening to this band of Germans rehearsing for a concert they were practicing for, where they were playing only Jewish music. It was hard for me to sit in that room without sobbing . . . I almost wanted to run out, but I suppressed my emotions and stayed in that room, to honour what they were doing. Here, the nation that treated my nation like absolute filth were honouring some of our traditions and culture as very precious and beautiful.

Next day I asked that German sister why they were playing Jewish music. Was it out of guilt? No! Not in the least! We are not guilty of what happened! We just discovered the music and loved it!

That touched me deeply. I would have hated them to be doing it out of guilt.

In the years that followed (23 of them so far) I visited my godchild and her family every single year without fail in the Black Forest and carried her on my shoulders till she became too heavy to carry. The two sisters have become my beloved German sisters, and I am at home with them as part of their family every year.

Such is my post-Holocaust experience!

I never asked them about "what did your parents do in the war?"

But they freely told me. It was not all good. Not all bad.

The Germans are not "different". They are typically human, as I said at the beginning.

It simply is not accurate to accuse a perpetrating nation of being more inherently evil than any other "good" or "god-fearing" nation. Their atrocities are expressions of being human, not just expressions of a particular nation or group. Oh, the situation, the current environment of the perpetrators might have predisposed them to commit their atrocities, but their heinous acts are part of the universal human armamentarium, to particular to their particular nation.

What I am suggesting is that the Ruandan genocide and Killing Fields of Cambodia, and the Nazi Holocaust, and all the many other mass massacres were carried out by humans, as humans.

Murder of the people, by the people, as the people!!!

Murder of humans, by humans, as humans!!!

We need to be careful that if we start designating one group as inherently evil that we are not guilty of the same process of projecting (inherent) evil onto a particular group which is what causes the problem in the first place.

This means that all and anyone has a right to ask all and anyone about the atrocities of their ancestors. Because all atrocities, all perpetrations, all murder of innocent people, especially of non-warring citizens, have no moral validity.

But when people don't want to look into the past of their direct ancestors, in whatever wars, whichever genocides, perhaps we should be at least a little pushy about asking them to confront the memories and atrocities of their grandparents . . . being sure to make them know that we know:

It was your grandfather and your nation that expressed these most primitive stupid destructive very universal human tendencies and caused endless sufferings thereby. At other times in history, other humans acted on the same destructive tendencies. In the future, yet other humans will do the same, unless . . .

At least, at this time in history, own up to your family's, or your nation's past.

Surely every nation and family should at least own up to their ancestors own destructive pasts?

The Old Testament commandments tells us that killing is wrong.

But in other parts, it revels in how many of the enemy were killed or died! Perhaps it was a jubilation because a

---

threat to our existence was neutralised. But if we were really godly, we should be mourning the achievement of our safety and peace . . .that there was a failure of human creativity, a defeat of human reconciliation, a failure of human love! That we could not agree on a different way of resolving this!

The only really constructive human victories are those when we can solve conflicts without killing each other.

Military victories are pale and primitive by comparison!

But planetary citizens are still a long way from learning how to do that, or even being motivated to that.

Of course, you may be one of these people who validates the primitive stupid behaviour of your nation's past, like "Hitler was right" or something like that.   If you are one of those stupid destructive human beings, well, for one thing, you are almost certainly not reading this book. Secondly, you truly are one of the humans who, if allowed to again, encouraged to again, will gladly perpetrate the same atrocities again on innocent victims. I hope there are few of you, and I hope all of us in society will work towards not ever letting such idiots as yourselves take over society and wreak havoc on innocent humans who you think are "not us" and who you think that, as "not us", they should be destroyed. When 2 Jews were killed in a hate crime in Germany recently, tens of thousands of Germans protested in Berlin that this racism and antisemitism is unacceptable! I replied on the Facebook post that reported that: "Modern Germany. I love you!".

So Dear non-Jewish Lithuanian descendants of perpetrators during the war, may I make an appeal, with kindness, compassion and understanding: Do find out if there were perpetrators in your ancestors! If they are still alive, please explain to them that they were total assholes — displaying primitive "unter-mensch" (in the Yiddish sense of "uncompassionate") type behaviour!!! Not very useful on the planet!

And, as long as you don't validate any of that past atrocious behaviour, we love you just the way you are. It has been touching here in the last months of the year 2019 that a video documentary entitled "The Lost Names of Lithuania" was produced. Lithuania is scattered with mass graves of un-named Jews, but we have records of most of them. So a group of people decided they would create a memorial wall to the fallen in a town called Birzai where the names of the known victims were inscribed. The numbers of local Lithuanian citizens who appeared for the ceremony was touching. And they all wore the yellow stars that were handed out, and walked the few kilometres from the town to the site where the local massacre of that town happened. There are about 200 or so of such mass grave sites in Lithuania.

THE HIDING OF CRIMES

There is another conundrum that keeps prodding my mind about my journey — which took in mainly the Nazi stupidities, but also the Russian stupidities after the war — the widespread atrocities of the KGB (Komitet gosudarstvennoy bezopasnosti —it should have been called the *Committee for State Insecurity* . . .because it made everyone in the state feel very insecure, was itself "the enemy within", but as this was in their own blindspot, could not see this and depicted themselves as fighting "the enemy within". There was none! They themselves were "the enemy within").

When I was at the KGB museum, in one of the prison cells in the whole prison area which covers the basement area, there was a pile of large sealed bags. The inscription on the door tells us that they were full of shredded records, as the KGB needed to hide their atrocities.

The Nazis too, were trying to hide their atrocities toward the end of the war, in many ways. One example was the death marches. By spreading dead bodies over miles and miles of road, it would ostensibly be hard for their conquerors to locate some kind of killing factories, as was the case with the concentration camps.

I wondered about this act by these nations to hide the evidence for their atrocities. Was there any shame or guilt involved??? Why do something if you cannot stand up proudly in front of the whole of humanity, and, in honour of all of humanity, commit to doing the thing that none of humanity would denunciate you for?   Why do something if you have to hide it?

Am I being naïve? Perhaps the reason nations hide their atrocities when they are losing is simply that they know they have "killed some enemy folk" and now, if discovered, will lead to "the enemy" killing them.

But if that were the case, then, if they are caught and tried anyway, they might as well argue in court that all they did was the right thing to do, in their eyes. Imagine! The Nurmberg trials . . .and a general arguing that, of course, it is the right thing to do to try and annihilate all the subhuman races on the planet, especially the Jews and Gypsies. A few did maintain their sick loyalty to Nazism as far as I can remember. Many of the lower rank Germans tried the defence of "I was just following orders". As I said, I would then want to know if you followed them willingly, or were totally against what was happening, but could do very little against it. Because it sure seems as if the Germans involved in the great Nazi victories at the beginning of the war were doing the murdering very happily and with great gusto, not with a sense of "this is awful, but we have to do this, or we will be killed too"

If perpetrators experience no shame or guilt for their murderous atrocities, they are basically living from a nihilistic philosophy that says "kill or be killed". No right or wrong here! Just survival of the fittest! No ethics! No morality! No love for humanity!

IN CONCLUSION

I appeal to the younger generations of my own family (and of all families) to take some time during their long lives to educate themselves at least basically on these, and all, Holocaust and genocide horrors. And also to know how many of their direct ancestors perished in those, and perhaps even to know their names, and to pass that on to coming generations. It is not a bad thing to do, not a waste of the present . . . though I know you, in your young years, like I did in mine, must concentrate on the urgent needs of the present, and on future goals.

We, the current older citizens of planet earth of this generation have "witnessed" a ton of genocidal action in our lifetime, and know about a ton of that from the 20th Century alone . . . Citizens, I appeal to you to use the history of the past to ensure that we have a different future and that truly *NEVER AGAIN* becomes a reality. It is up to every one of us . . . to join the good fight against our own human destructiveness.

So, here are some of my last messages I would like to leave you with:

I think we should never think that the violent nature of perpetrators of atrocious attacks on the bodies of their victims comes from the race, religion, nation, group, or ideology that perpetrate them. The violent nature comes from being human! We should never identify this violent nature as being the unique and special part of any identifiable group. The group that has this nature is called: "Humanity"

Don't fear the big bombs inside the military arsenals.

The big bombs are inside human beings.

If we don't defuse them there, we are lost!

If we succeed in defusing them there, we can joyfully celebrate the winning of this very different, but very quintessential war against unbelievable human stupidity in allowing the lowest parts of our natures to reign.

And . . . by the way!

This is the grave situation of my Lithuanian ancestors:

Not a single one has their own grave or gravestone!

The haters wanted a total wipe-out —hence no gravestones to remember the dead.

I offer these writings as one epitaph for those non-existent gravestones.

Aron Gersh

London

12 August 2019

<u>That Ed McCurdy poem</u>

<u>on the first page carries on like this:</u>

For Love exists! It always has!

It is for you! It is for me!

And if we stop denying it

We all together may agree

To search each other out

And find a peaceful destiny

For if we don't, and still go on

With slaughter, hate and pain,

The Agony will never end

And nothing will remain

. . .

"Love is Wise. Hatred is foolish."

— Bertrand Russell

THE AUTHOR

I am from a generation of Jewish children born post WWII in South Africa most of whose parents were immigrants from Lithuania before the war. Their mother-tongue was Yiddish, and they spoke English with a funny, recognisable accent which we children do not have, but often mimic jokingly.

Not being very happy living in the cruelty of Apartheid South Africa, I went to live in London when I was 31 years old and have lived there half my life.

I trained as a Humanistic Psychologist at Antioch University, USA, when it had a branch in London, England, for 10 years. I then worked as a psychotherapist for eight years after which I ran a quarterly psychology magazine, entitled *Human Potential,* for eight more years. Have published two books in the last 2 years on the subject of the psychology of romantic love —about why love often fails, and what constitutes real true love (as opposed to fantasy "true love"). The longer book is entitled *Falling for Love,* and its shorter version, which summarises its main thesis, is called *The Soulmate Illusion.*

I am committed to the proposition that the psychology of war is humankind's biggest pathology, biggest psychological sickness, and that if we don't deal with the human nature that predisposes humans so easily to war, we will never solve the problem of war. I am now committed to lifelong study of this and hope to make valuable contributions to this before I die (hopefully in about 25 years' time —dying, I mean, not "making a contribution"). Thank you for reading, and please contribute to growing human compassion and emotional intelligence (Love for Humanity) both in yourselves and in others.

www.ingramcontent.com/pod-product-compliance
Lightning Source LLC
Chambersburg PA
CBHW070634030426
42337CB00020B/4007